# GIRLHOOD

P9-DYJ-425

# GIRLHOOD

## TEENS AROUND THE WORLD
## IN THEIR
## OWN VOICES

**Langley-Adams Library**
Groveland, MA
langleyadamslib.org

## MASUMA AHUJA

### ALGONQUIN 2021

ING
3/21

Published by Algonquin Young Readers
an imprint of Algonquin Books of Chapel Hill
Post Office Box 2225
Chapel Hill, North Carolina 27515-2225

a division of Workman Publishing
225 Varick Street
New York, New York 10014

© 2021 by Masuma Ahuja.
All rights reserved.
Printed in South Korea.
Published simultaneously in Canada by Thomas Allen & Son Limited.
Design by Kayla E.

Library of Congress Cataloging-in-Publication Data
Names: Ahuja, Masuma, 1989– author.
Title: Girlhood : teens around the world in their own voices / Masuma Ahuja.
Description: First edition. | Chapel Hill, North Carolina : Algonquin Young Readers, 2021. | Includes bibliographical references. | Audience: Ages 12 and up | Audience: Grades 7–9 | Summary: "Journalist Masuma Ahuja introduces us to 30 teenage girls from 27 countries. Through diary entries and photographs, they share their own stories of growing up and show what ordinary girlhood is like all over the world"—Provided by publisher.
Identifiers: LCCN 2020020764 | ISBN 9781643750118 (trade paperback) | ISBN 9781643751221 (ebook)
Subjects: LCSH: Teenage girls—Social conditions—Cross-cultural studies—Juvenile literature. | Girls—Social conditions—Cross-cultural studies—Juvenile literature.
Classification: LCC HQ798 .A555 2021 | DDC 305.235/2—dc23
LC record available at https://lccn.loc.gov/2020020764

10 9 8 7 6 5 4 3 2 1
First Edition

3 2121 00087 1547

For my parents, who always
taught me that I could be any
type of girl I wanted to be.

# Contents

VARVARA

SATTIGUL
AYAULYM

HALIMA
RUKSAR

RUOXIAO*

DIZA

CHANLEAKNA*
RAKSA

CHEN XI

CLAUDIE

ANNA

CHANLEAKNA*

NAYA*

MIRIAM

AMIYA
RUOXIAO*
MARTA

HALIMA

NAYA*

RUQAYA
DESIREÉ

FAVOUR

JOCELYNE

VIONA

MANDISA

EMMA

SHANAI
SOPHIE

LUCIANA

MERISENA

SOFIA

EMILLY
ALEJANDRA

*Some of the girls live or have lived in more than one country.

# Introduction

CHEN XI STAYS UP all night studying for a test. Miriam has butterflies in her stomach every time she talks to her crush. Merisena worries about her father getting hurt when he leaves for work. This is what girlhood looks like around the world.

I asked thirty girls whose lives span twenty-seven countries to share diary entries and a few photos with us. I wanted to see their world through their eyes, and in their own words.

These are their stories about what it looks like to be a teenage girl moving through ordinary life in different contexts and circumstances, often at the edge of the headlines we read in the news. What does it mean to grow up in a family that had to flee a war? What do you dream of when you grow up in poverty? What is it like to raise a child as a teen mom? To deal with mental illness or eating disorders? What does it mean to navigate a crush or a breakup with your boyfriend or girlfriend? To balance friendship and fun with endless hours of homework and pressure to achieve? To figure out who you are and how to be a girl and a woman in our world, in the age of Instagram and Boko Haram?

If you go by the numbers from 2015 to 2018, this is what a portrait of girlhood around the world looks like:

• One in five girls around the world marries before the age of 18.[1] In fact, every single day, 41,000 girls under the age of 18 marry.[2]
• Every year, an estimated 16 million girls between the ages of 15 and 19 give birth.[3]
• About 130 million girls between the ages of 6 and 17 are not in school. Their parents might need them to work, they might be living in a place where it's not safe to go to school because of violence, or they might be married or be mothers who are expected to stay home and take care of the family instead of going to school.[4]

These facts paint a dark and dire picture, showing how the simple fact of being a girl can be political, and the many ways in which girls are silenced or policed. They highlight the prevalence of violence, repression, or abuse that girls face just because they are girls; laws that limit girls' rights; and cultures that dictate how girls are allowed to dress, act, or live.

For example, in India and China, there are millions of "missing girls"—female fetuses are sometimes aborted because boys are preferred, or girls are neglected because families give more attention and resources to boys. In Afghanistan, millions of girls are out of school because of ongoing conflict, as schools have been bombed and burned, teachers abducted and attacked. In parts of Nigeria, girls have been abducted while going to school. Until 2020, in Tanzania, Equatorial Guinea, and Sierra Leone— all countries in sub-Saharan Africa, which has the highest rate of adolescent pregnancy—girls were banned by law from going to school after they had children. These conditions aren't limited to just Africa and Asia. In the United States, between 2010 and 2018, about 250,000 children under the age of 18 married; some were as young as 12 years old, and most of them were girls. Since 2016, states have started passing laws to ban child marriage, but many still do not have such laws on the books.[5]

There are other important ways in which girls around the world are restricted. Cultures keep them off sports fields, and communities dissuade them from pursuing education and ambitious dreams.

These facts define the circumstances within which girls live, but beyond these headlines and circumstances, we rarely hear from girls themselves about what life is like for them.

We do get to see, on the other end of the spectrum, pieces of life from influencers—filtered updates, curated posts, life in snippets. Not the ordinary, humdrum stuff that fills most people's days but never makes their feeds.

I wanted to know: What does a girl growing up in Iraq dream of? What does a girl in New York or Nigeria stay up nights thinking about? How would the story of girlhood be told if girls were the ones to write it?

The only way to find out, of course, was to ask girls themselves. So that is what I did.

This question led to a series I wrote for the *Washington Post*'s *The Lily*, which featured twelve girls from ten different countries. This book was born from that series.

I gave each girl instructions for writing diary entries, but then I encouraged them to ignore those instructions and follow their instincts. I wanted to know what was on their minds, how they were spending their days, and how they were feeling.

Some girls had never written a diary entry before. Some girls chose instead to message me at the end of every day with updates. And others shared photos of journals they'd been keeping since childhood.

Because I asked for written entries, I could only include girls who have learned how to write and are comfortable with words. And these pages only feature girls who were able to share and who felt safe sharing their stories. How much and what you will read about each girl's life was up to her. Each girl decided what to share with us, and how she would like to be represented. While the diary entries have been lightly edited for length and clarity, and some have been translated from their original language, they are all the work of the girls I interviewed.

To accompany each girl's diary entries, I have researched and written about the context of her life—about her community, her circumstances, the themes she explores, or the country in which she lives—to help you better understand the slice of life that each girl shares with us.

This book could not be comprehensive—there are more than a billion girls in the world, each with her own voice and her own story, and this is not an atlas of girlhood, after all—but I hope it is representative of a vast range of girls' experiences.

Despite the differences of where they live, there is so much of life that looks the same across latitudes and longitudes, across borders and oceans: the daily moments of worrying about homework or laughing with friends, parents who just don't understand them, and plotting big dreams for the future. The girls explore what it's like to feel like an outsider, to find friends and communities who understand them, to experience leaving home, and the ways in which they're trying to make their plans and dreams come true. I hope the range of stories will help you see the different ways in which girls are navigating similar challenges as they begin to make sense of themselves and the world.

As I put this book together, I thought often about the only experience of girlhood that I am intimately familiar with: my own. My teenage years were split across three continents, and I rarely encountered stories like mine in popular culture. I read a lot growing up, but there were so few books about girls whose lives looked anything like mine. I caught glimpses in places, but they were rare. So I spent many of my teenage years explaining my other homes to people who often had only a few cultural references or stereotypes—America is like *Friends* and the Baby-Sitters Club, and India is the land of snake charmers. But in reality, life was so much more than any of these stereotypes or single stories.

In putting together this book, I found echoes of the emotions and types of experiences of my own teenage years. While the specifics of each life are different—and make for colorful and rich stories—many of the themes that teenage girls experience and explore are similar: a longing for the adventures ahead, dreams burning big and bright, and the angst and growing pains of figuring out their own place in the world.

I hope that as you read these stories and are transported around the globe, you find glimpses of yourself in unexpected corners, too. ◊

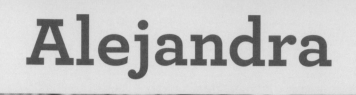

# Alejandra

**17**
years old

Buenos Aires, Argentina

## What do you want to do when you grow up?

I want to travel, to pursue the career that I am going to study. At this moment I am deciding whether to choose medicine with specialization in traumatology [a branch of medicine that focuses on injuries after trauma, such as violence or accidents] or odontology [a branch of medicine like dentistry, which is the study of teeth].

## How do you like to spend your time when you're not in school?

I like to move, go to the field, go for a walk, run, ride a bike, go to a friend's house or have a friend come over to my place, listen to music in my room, play with my brothers. Or I'll spend some time with my mother and father, either go shopping or go to the square [a public space in the city] with my family for a while.

I love doing sports; I like all of them. I do not like being locked up at home, not that I have anything against my family, but I feel suffocated and I need to go for a walk in the neighborhood at least.

## Are there any particular activities that you enjoy?

I train [for soccer] 2 or 3 times a week and we have tournaments on weekends. I have also been doing photography courses for two years.

## Tell us about your friends.

I am a very social person; I have friends everywhere. Real friends, I do not really have many. I've had experiences where I enjoyed individual people, but in the end they did not turn out to be who I thought they were. But it's a good part of the life experience. I know that I have people to tell if something happens to me. I know I'm not alone.

But the concept of a best friend doesn't apply. Maybe because I still haven't met someone like that. I'm young, soon I'll be 18, and I know that many people are waiting for me to meet them.

# "On the field we are all partners, we are sisters who share many things."

**"I WOULD LOVE** to be able to play football wherever I am," Alejandra says, "My dream is to travel with a camera and a ball."

She's grown up in a country that's known for its soccer team—the men's team has won the World Cup twice. In fact, you can find Argentinean soccer fans in countries across the globe, in their blue-and-white striped jerseys, cheering for Argentine players Lionel Messi or Diego Maradona, two of the world's most famous footballers (as they're called outside the United States).

But what is it like to be a girl, and a soccer player, in a country with such vibrant soccer fandom and culture? Alejandra's life in Buenos Aires gives us a peak into this world. She grew up watching boys and men playing soccer,

Buenos Aires,
Argentina

**ALEJANDRA PLAYS** on a girls' soccer team set up by La Nuestra, or La Nuestra Fútbol Femenino. This group uses soccer to help promote gender equality and fight gender-based violence, and it's one of many larger efforts across the country. As recently as June 2019, thousands of women in Argentina organized and took to the streets to protest the high rate of violence against women in the country.[6]

The data on gender-based violence in Argentina is staggering. The rate of femicide (the murder of women and girls because of their gender) is very high, and statistics suggest that one woman is murdered there about every 32 hours.[7] In 2017, the country's Unique Registry for Cases of Violence Against Women documented more than 85,000 reports.[8] ◊

and eventually, with a little fear and a lot of encouragement from her family, she decided to give the sport a try too.

Alejandra writes about the sisterhood and friendship she's found on the team. She writes about how her teammates support each other on the field and off, the friendship she's found with her brother and in her family, and the ways in which she's longed for a best friend, the kind you see in movies.

Our friendships, especially in our teenage years, can be such a powerful force. They help shape the people we become and the ways in which we understand the world. ◊

Translated
from Spanish

*April 20*

My morning involved house cleaning with my whole family. As I helped my mom, dad, and uncle, I watched the girls play in the women's lightning tournament* organized by the neighborhood girls on Saturday mornings until 2 p.m. The men's lightning tournament takes place almost every weekend and runs until midnight or later.

Today I could not participate in the tournament because I did not sign up and because I had to help at home.

In the afternoon, we watched my dad and one of my uncles, who is a goalkeeper, playing in the men's tournament.

When night came, I went to my friend's house and bought empanadas, gummies, and chocolate, and decided to go to the terrace to spend part of the night. I haven't seen her for a long time, and I missed her. I've known her for about two years, and I really love her. Since I met her, she has been there when I needed her, and whenever I want to do something, she accompanies me, and I her.

I think that in my 17, almost 18 years, my friendships have been few, but unique. I don't share the best friend label you give to someone else, at least not so far, maybe because I haven't found "my best friend." I think that is like what happens in movies. The friends I have and whom I really consider to be real friends are few. I try to get along well with all the people I know or who are around me, to be friendly and be there when

---

\* Lightning rounds are often shorter matches. In tournaments,
lightning rounds allow more teams to play in a short amount of time.

they need me. I like to do it, and the truth is that I do not expect anything in return, but well, there is always someone who will not like you.

So I prefer to enjoy the moment, have no hard feelings, laugh with everyone, listen to those who need it and try to help them. If I need someone to talk to, I know that some people are going to be willing to listen to me, some friends who will always cheer me up, my cousins who are always here to listen to me or accompany me somewhere, but mainly my family.

[There's] my mom, who I fight or argue with a lot. Since we are very similar in character, we do not like to lose in anything so in fights sometimes it is chaos because neither of us wants to give in . . . [but] our relationship never lacks hugs and apologies. At first I refused to accept the resemblance . . . She is always in a hurry and has a thousand things to do, but when it comes to us there is nothing else; if some neighbor or family friend needs something, she is there. She tries to emit joy throughout her day, starts singing at home; with my little brother, she makes jokes at any moment.

I share great and pleasant conversations with my dad in the car while he takes me to school and then goes to work . . . we have very different views on many things and sometimes it's hard to make him understand my reasons but at least he tries. Many times he tells us his stories from the past, and something always makes us laugh, they are often sad, but he always tries to leave us with some lesson.

My older brother . . . since he started college, I almost do not see him anymore. He is studying, or at his girlfriend's house, or with friends.

We always talk about a million things. Apart from being siblings, we are very good friends, and we have many things in common which makes it twice as interesting each time we talk. We can spend hours and hours talking and the topics of conversation do not end until one of us remembers that we have things to do the next day and we need to sleep. He is always willing to help me however he can, and he listens to me above all. Whenever I tell him something that makes me feel bad, he hugs me.

And my little brother is always there making me laugh or angry, just making me forget about everything else. He is a beautiful beast. Since he learned to stand, everything was revolutionized in my house. Since he learned to walk, he practically does not walk, he runs from when he gets up until he falls asleep. He talks, screams in every moment, and there are things that he says that make me totally surprised. Every day he's bigger, more awake, and more restless. He likes to go out; all the neighbors know him.

No matter what, he is happy being away from home, he runs behind Pol, our dog, runs with him all over the block, over and over, back and forth, laughing and screaming. Inside the house is the same. Whenever he is with the dog he wants to play or bother him. He is very affectionate, and if he sees you, many times he goes and asks you for a hug, he tells you "I love you" and gives you a kiss.

*April 23*

After four days of holidays and a weekend, I returned to the routine. I arrived at school, and I found out that the chemistry teacher had resigned. That improved my morning, I did not like to have classes with her at all, not because of the subject, but for how the teacher taught it. We had a new teacher, whom I liked, and I really got a good first impression, so I hope I'm not mistaken.

I like to go to school, I want to have classes; if we have free hours I get bored. I would like to study medicine, if I study this I would like to specialize in traumatology. I like the type of work they do, I have seen it up close with so many injuries that I had playing ball, doing another sport, or simply because of how awkward I am.

How nice to get home and that my mother welcomes me with a plate of homemade food. After lunch, I did a bit of schoolwork. After taking a little nap, I got up because it was time to go train.

Sometimes I arrive late, but that is my role in the group, being late always and everywhere. I do not say it proudly, but I accept it. I am unpunctual, but I try to be as responsible as possible. I'm working on changing that, I do not like it, but many times there are other factors that I don't take into account, like traffic, or the odd thing to do at the last moment as I leave at home. Yes, I know, I'm a disaster.

At practice, after hearing an instruction from Juli many times and trying it, today I was able to do it correctly. I have a weak kick when I hit the ball, but seconds before, a thought passes through my head that I have heard a million times from Juli, "To hit the ball hard, you make your abs firm, the strength comes from there accompanied with the movement of both legs: the one that steps firmly to give it direction and the other with the movement accompanied by the whole body," and *bam* I hit the ball. It worked well and it was not by accident, I felt good about myself and in a certain way proud, much more so when I hear her words of congratulation.

I often think about what would have happened if I, at 8 years old, had not wanted to play football like my dad or my older brother. At first, I only saw them from home, I saw how the kids got out on the field to play and train, I saw more and more girls of all ages coming. I was encouraged to go out to play with them. At first I was afraid, of not knowing how to play, of not knowing them, for being small and for my physique.

I started to go out more often as the days went by. I really felt comfortable with the support of my coaches, Juliana and Mónica, who took care of the bigger girls but who were also with us.

I also had great support from my mom and dad, who told me, "If all those girls are playing, why are you not going to be able to do it?" So with time I left the fears I had behind and I was able to play freely, play in a place where we are all equal, where size, color, physicality, sexuality, or tastes do not make a difference. On the field we are all partners, we

are sisters who share many things, from training, matches, tournaments,
chores, birthdays, in-depth conversations full of emotions, joys, feelings
of pride, sadness, tears, and above all laughs and smiles.

Every day we learn something new, which can be something
technical or something for our lives.

*Thank you to La Nuestra Fútbol Femenino for connecting me with Alejandra.*

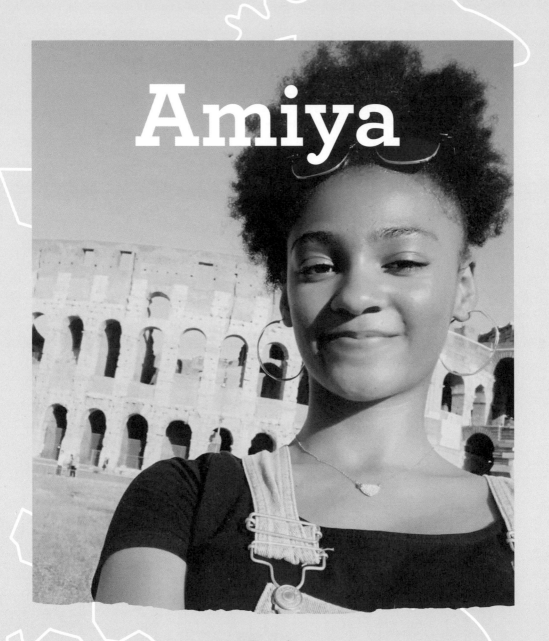

# Amiya

## 14
### years old

London, United Kingdom

## What music do you like?

Pink Floyd, The Beatles, The Rolling Stones, Queen, and AC/DC are among my favourite bands. I also listen to some '90s music here and there, like Nirvana or Nine Inch Nails or TLC. Duran Duran is my fave band from the '80s.

## What are your favorite films?

*The Breakfast Club*, *Sixteen Candles*, *Beetlejuice*, *Heathers*, and *Back to the Future*. I think, at times, that I was born in the wrong generation. I'm an '80s kid at heart.

## What are your favorite subjects?

History. I love to learn about different societies through time and how mankind has evolved over the last millennia.

## Tell us about your best friends.

I've had the same best friend since 2017. Her name's Sadja. She really likes Eminem (the rapper). I've got another best friend who's a boy, and his name's Hassan. He likes watching anime and playing video games. I've got two other close friends, Zenab and Marwa. Zenab's a talented artist, and Marwa is addicted to Netflix.

# "Everyone in this black-and-white world seems to solely focus on the negatives, and it seriously bugs me."

**AMIYA IS FOURTEEN** and a half years old and lives in London, one of the most vibrant cities in the world. She describes her neighborhood as one that's both close to the bustle of the city and also where foxes roam at night. She lives around the corner from a big park that fills up with children in the summertime. Her neighborhood was bombed heavily during World War II, so many houses, including hers, were rebuilt in the late 1940s.

Amiya has a close-knit family and she lives with her mother, stepfather, younger brothers, and cat. While she doesn't live with her biological father, they remain close and she sees him regularly.

"When I'm not at school, I typically attend my swim classes and my Chinese kickboxing classes. I meet up with my friends every now and then, and we'll go to the cinema or go shopping," she says. Her interests both inside and outside school are wide-ranging. She loves law, sociology, criminology, astrophysics, ballet, writing, and swimming.

In one of her diary entries, Amiya writes about wanting to be an astrophysicist. But when I ask her what she dreams of doing when she grows up, she says, "I don't necessarily know what I want to do when I grow up. I love a variety of things . . . it's too hard to choose now."

When she was younger, Amiya wanted to become an actress. "At some point, I enrolled in Sylvia Young, a renowned drama school in central London. But then I stopped going. I'm currently trying to look for acting classes but they're all very expensive," she says. ◊

London,
United Kingdom

**AMIYA LIVES IN** a very diverse city and a country that's growing increasingly racially diverse. She's one of 1.2 million people—about two percent of the population—in England who identify as multiracial, according to the 2011 census.[9]

But what does that mean for Amiya's daily life?

In one diary entry, Amiya starts to describe a trip to a beauty shop to buy hair product, but it turns into a thoughtful exploration on race, identity, and otherhood. She writes eloquently about growing up in a world where Western beauty standards and culture often mean that hair like hers isn't seen as beautiful or professional. And about the specific experience of not being treated with respect and feeling like she's being treated like an "other"—a curiosity, instead of an equally respected person—when strangers touch her hair.

In Amiya's words, "I'm not an animal in London Zoo, thank you very much, I am a human being."

Amiya isn't alone in her experience. Many black women in the UK and other countries deal with judgment and the policing of their hair. Pop music star Solange perhaps said it best, in a 2016 interview with NPR about her song "Don't Touch My Hair." "Black hair has such a significance in black culture. And also, it's such an insular experience. Growing up, being a young girl, transitioning to junior high school, then into adulthood, the hair journey of a black woman is so specific, and it's really hard. Your hair can send so many different messages to so many different people in the world that it becomes political. It becomes social . . . It encompasses a much bigger conversation of appropriation, of ownership, of protected space."[10] ◊

Dear Diary,

Today I woke up not feeling like myself. For some reason, I feel so unhappy. And the worst thing is, I have no real reason to feel like this. I know that I live in a great place with a ton of opportunities, and I have a beautiful home, a nice big garden, two pets, electronics, and a functional loving family. I just don't know why I feel so sad. Maybe it's because every day is a repeat of the last.

I wake up to the sound of my Echo Dot, 6 a.m. sharp every morning. I go through my daily hygiene routine, ride my bike, get dressed, feed my cat, walk down the road to the bus stop, wait a couple of minutes for the big red bus to approach, which will take me straight to the place I'll spend the next 8 systematic hours of my life.

Of course, I should be grateful for the great educational system I've been born into, blah blah blah . . . I hear all the time from teachers that I should feel grateful that I've got a free education. I am grateful. Never said I wasn't. I don't consider myself a spoilt brat. But that doesn't necessarily mean I should always be content with the teaching with a big smile on my face, and act like some clone of happiness.

I come home and I binge-watch some shows on Netflix and hear my parents moaning about chores I haven't done in the house.

What about the things I have done? No one ever drones on for hours on end about that.

Everyone in this black-and-white world seems to solely focus on the negatives, and it seriously bugs me.

Dear Diary,

I cleaned my room today, turns out I own hundreds of clothes I've never worn, and some I never knew even existed. Also, I actually managed to leave the house today. Whoopee! A beautiful, glistening gold medal for my fantastic achievement. At around 6 p.m., as the rain was pelting down from the sky like literal bullets, I got on the bus down the road to a hair centre that also specializes in beauty cosmetics. I bought some hair stuff from there: flexi rods, Cantu curl activator cream, and some Australian mousse. I've always struggled with my really thick hair since I was a little girl, so I'm always having to buy new products and test them out. At times, I wished I was born with curly hair that all the other mixed race girls have. The hair that's both admired and accepted. It came to the point where 5 years ago, when I was in year 5 or 6 in primary school, I actually used a permanent relaxer in my hair; I regret that stupid decision of mine till this day. But hey, silly decisions are there to be a lesson for whenever I plan on doing something idiotic like using chemicals in my hair again.

I was born with an afro and I must embrace it, because that's how God intended it to be. I may occasionally feel like the odd one out, but that's who I am. I'm Amiya. I'm mixed-race, biracial, polyethnic, multiracial, "half-caste," whatever you want to call it (but not half-caste because I find it incredibly offensive), and I'm PROUD to be . . . Finally.

It's also made me realise that as black women—and black men, too—we're constantly put down because of our hair unless it's conventionally straight or curly. It's bloody irritating. Why is straight European/Asian hair only socially accepted, yet black hair is seen as being "too political" or "not professional enough." Oh, I'm ever-so sorry, I didn't know that my culture isn't acceptable enough for some. My tight coils must be affecting them so much that they simply can't go about their day without making a comment about how "I should straighten it" or "wash it more often so that the ringlets are much more defined and not so nappy."

And I find it very rude when people just touch my hair without my permission. I'm not an animal in London Zoo, thank you very much, I am a human being. Sure, they may not realise what they're doing, and I get it—black hair is fascinating and different to those who are not accustomed to it. But still don't touch it.

✳ ✳ ✳

Dear Diary,

I want to become an astrophysicist when I'm older, but I'm worried I won't be able to be because of my poor maths grade. I excel in science, yet my maths is diabolical (it doesn't make any sense). It's terrible. Physics is heavily related to maths yet I'm so laughably bad at it it hurts.

I don't just pass all my subjects at school, I excel at them. But maths is the only thing letting my report down. I've been revising maths much more recently and going over my weakest subjects. But no matter what I do, including all this extra work I put in, I just can't seem to achieve higher than 30% in any one of my mathematical tests. Even my friends get higher than me, and it makes no sense because I put in a lot more effort than them.

My dad and grandma keep saying they want to get me a maths tutor and I'm glad they want to help me. But my grandma is living in Africa right now with my Ghanaian family, so it'll be hard for her to get me a tutor halfway across the world. My dad's a major procrastinator so I doubt it'll ever happen from him.

# Anna

## 14
### years old

Sydney, Australia

**What are your favorite subjects?**
English, history, Latin, and Mandarin

**What are your favorite books?**
It's a long list, but they include a collection of Jane Austen's works, *Anna and the Swallow Man* by Gavriel Savit, *Anna Karenina* by Leo Tolstoy, *The Great Gatsby* by F. Scott Fitzgerald, *To Kill a Mockingbird* by Harper Lee, *Les Miserables* by Victor Hugo, *Useless Magic* by Florence Welch (the singer from Florence and the Machine, my favorite band).

You may also notice the doll in the picture—I've had her since I was 3— she's Alice, from *Alice in Wonderland,* one of my favorite children's books.

> "Learning a language is similar to the feeling I get from solving a puzzle—you can arrange words in different ways to create different meanings."

**WHEN I ASKED ANNA** about herself, she shared a long list of her favorite books—from Jane Austen's novels to *Anna Karenina*. Books are central to her life. Even her dog is named Boo Radley, after a character in *To Kill a Mockingbird*, a book she loves.

Anna lives in Australia with her parents, who are both doctors in the same hospital (and who, she's quick to note, also love to read); her younger brother; and her dog. She spends her days going to school, spending time with family, doing homework, going to piano lessons ("I love to play the piano, but have no natural talent," she says), and reading books.

Anna says she doesn't know exactly "who or what I want to be when I'm older" but shared a list of the things she is certain about:

• I want to write and publish poetry, or a novel.
• I want to be bilingual (or possibly trilingual).
• I want to help people (cliché as it sounds).

"As you've probably guessed, I absolutely love literature," she says. "I also love languages."

Anna writes with curiosity and enthusiasm about exploring her hometown and places beyond it. For Anna, understanding the world and her place in it comes primarily through the words she reads and writes.

Through the words she shares, Anna gives us a peak into her world, and how she travels to other worlds—through the books she reads, the languages she learns, and the dreams she builds. ◊

Sydney,
Australia

**ANNA HAS GROWN UP** in Sydney, a multicultural coastal city that is dotted with more than one hundred beaches.[11] Her family lives close to Sydney Harbor, in a house where you can see the water from almost every room.

The city is also incredibly diverse: about 40 percent of people who live in Sydney were born in a country other than Australia, and about the same percentage of people speak languages other than English at home—with Mandarin, Arabic, Cantonese, Vietnamese, and Greek being some of the most common.[12] In all, more than 250 languages are spoken in Sydney.[13]

Growing up in this diverse city with a grandparent who speaks another language, Anna writes about her own love for words and her efforts, both in school and on her own, to learn other languages. She takes Latin and Mandarin in school, and she's also tried to teach herself some Greek to be able to talk to her grandfather. He moved to Australia from Lesbos, Greece, when he was just a teenager. ◊

*Saturday*

Today, I woke up early, and listened to the rain, drifting in and out of sleep. After showering and eating breakfast with my mother and brother, I spent the day doing homework. I didn't really have that much to do, just maths exercises, work from science and geography, a history essay to finish, and the Mandarin test to study for. However, I am notoriously good at wasting time—I don't know how or why, but somehow everything I try to accomplish takes so much longer than I originally planned.

I did, however, manage to spend time doing things I enjoy. Every weekend, a friend and I have a tradition of calling each other and talking about our week. We met through our younger brothers—they became close friends, and now we're close friends.

I also spent time reading. I will admit that I do not spend as much time reading as I did when I was younger; the high school workload has devoured my free time, and I feel my attention span is slowly shortening. (I can be quite melodramatic sometimes . . .) The book I'm reading is dark and interesting and arty.

My grandfather ate dinner with my family this evening. He was born in Lesbos, Greece, and migrated to Australia when he was 16. I've tried to teach myself Greek, so I can have more in common with him, but I only know simple phrases (*Hello, how are you? What did you do today?*) and I can read the alphabet. It's a start, if nothing else.

After dinner, my brother and I ate way too much chocolate and binge-watched television together. I am an absolute hypocrite—complain about not having enough time to read, and will then waste an hour in front of the television . . .

It's 9:45 p.m. I'm going to get to sleep.

※　※　※

*Sunday*

I set an alarm for 6:45 so I could wake up and get my homework over and done with. I finished my science homework, and then my family and I walked to a local café for breakfast. Afterwards, I began my history homework. I'm probably giving the representation that I have a lot of homework, and I do, but keep in mind that I'm incredibly inefficient . . .

At around 11:30, my dad drove me to a friend's place. We're working on our English assignment together and decided to meet up over the weekend to make some progress on it. We had originally planned to go ice-skating afterwards, but unfortunately, we didn't have enough time. Nevertheless, it was a fun afternoon: we worked on the balcony, drank tea, and played with her cat. Her parents prepared an incredible two-course lunch. At 3:30, my dad picked me up and took me home. In our front garden, we have two olive trees (hearkening back to our Greek heritage). I helped pick some olives, then my father brined them.

I practiced piano and became too intimidated to begin studying for the Mandarin test. Instead, I decided to read. I ate dinner with my family, then washed the dishes with my father and brother.

We finished the movie we began watching last night, and now here I am. I'm supposed to be asleep, but I think I'll stay up and try to write poetry.

※ ※ ※

*Monday*

Today was stressful because I realized that we had a lot less time to work on the English assignment than I previously thought. The first lesson of the day was Mandarin. Learning a language is similar to the feeling I get from solving a puzzle (once again, a cliché)—you can arrange words in different ways to create different meanings.

Next, we had a library lesson. We have these once every fortnight. I found an interesting book—it's written in the style of a gothic novel. After recess, I had geography and science. Lunch was relaxing, I planned to get some work done, but instead spent it with friends. Our final class was sport. We spent the lesson swimming laps in the school pool. I spent the afternoon doing homework in my dressing gown. I revised [studied] for the Mandarin test, and added to an essay for history. I finished at around 8:30 p.m. I spend the majority of Monday evenings alone whilst my mother takes my brother to tutoring. I like the novelty of being alone—I'm not exactly sure why though. I stayed up past my bedtime reading.

# Ayaulym

## 19
### years old

Almaty, Kazakhstan

### What kinds of movies do you like?

Mostly I like to watch documentaries, or films based on real events. I am also a fan of the Marvel Universe. When I watch these films, I begin to believe in miracles. I always buy a ticket for Marvel films in advance, and I don't miss any movies.

### What are your favorite books?

My favorite book is *The Alchemist* by Paulo Coelho. I read this book three times, and each time it opened more and more for me. I also love his other books.

### What are your favorite subjects?

All the subjects that I study at the university are very interesting to me, but my favorite subject is Science of Culture.

# "I like to watch documentaries, or films based on real events. I am also a fan of the Marvel Universe. When I watch these films, I begin to believe in miracles."

Almaty, Kazakhstan

**AYAULYM LOVES TO READ.** She just finished *A Tree Grows in Brooklyn* and is about to start *The Da Vinci Code*. She also loves going to the cinema and taking walks in the park.

Like many of the girls in this book—including Sattigul in Mongolia and Raksa in Cambodia—Ayaulym has to leave her home and live in a dormitory in another city in order to attend university. She travels from her village, Tonkeris, to Almaty Technology University in Almaty, one of Kazakhstan's largest cities. At home, she lives with her mother (a teacher) and her father (a nurse). She is the youngest of three sisters; the older two are both married with children.

Ayaulym is studying the restaurant and hotel business. After college, she hopes to get a job in a restaurant or hotel. "I want to better tourism in our country . . . In this way, I can help develop our country's economy," she says.

Ayaulym spends most of her spare time in the dorm, chatting with the other girls who live there. Some of them, like Ayaulym, are from villages in other parts of the country, but many are international students. In fact, in 2018, there were 18,000 international students in Kazakhstan.[14] Many were from countries in Central Asia, India, and China, and some were from as far away as Mexico.[15] ◊

**KAZAKHSTAN WAS** part of the Soviet Union, a region stretching from Eastern Europe across Russia that was governed from Moscow under a communist regime from 1922 to 1991. Kazakhstan is a big country—about the size of Western Europe—and it has one of the biggest economies in Central Asia.[16] Its wealth is driven mostly by oil and minerals.

It ranks 52 out of 144 countries on the global gender gap index,[17] which measures inequality between men and women across different areas, including job opportunities, how men and women are comparatively paid for doing the same jobs, and how many women are in political office. ◊

Translated
from Russian

*May 15, 2019*

Today was a very good day; I think the weather contributed to that.

I woke up today at 7:00 a.m. and went for a run; every day my result is better, and there are more and more people in the stadium. Then at 7:40 a.m. I came home, took a shower, and made a tasty breakfast. I love breakfasts.

Tomorrow is my sister Nurzhamal's birthday; she lives in Astana. And today I bought a plane ticket online. I will fly there on the 21st of May. I think she will be really excited about my arrival, because she has been trying to convince me to come to her for 5 years.

Today, I finished reading a novel *A Tree Grows in Brooklyn*, a very interesting book. I enjoyed it. Now it is the turn of *The Da Vinci Code*. I have heard a lot about this book, and I think it will be interesting.

Then I practiced English for an hour. When will I learn the whole English grammar?! :(

I waited for my nephew after school, and we worked on his homework. Since I am now on holiday, I try to make more time for him.

We finished the day by riding bikes.

Dad taught me to ride a bike from an early age, so now I ride very well.

In general, I had a nice day. I'm going to bed. It's 11:00 p.m.

*May 16, 2019*

Today was a great day. Because it was my mom's birthday. She turned 51. We celebrated with the people we are closest to.

Preparation began in the morning. Since it is now the holy month of Ramadan, we invited guests to dinner in the evening. Only the closest [were invited], and it was about 30 people, if not more LOL.

The sisters came with their husbands and children, grandparents, all my cousins and dad's brothers. We had a great time with the family. There was a lot of food and a lot of hearty talk.

We sat until midnight. Then we started cleaning and gave all the guests treats. So that was mom's birthday.

✳ ✳ ✳

*May 17, 2019*

Today was a very productive day.

I ran in the morning, 2 laps more than usual. I woke up at 7:00 a.m. I came home, took a shower, and ate a tasty breakfast.

Then I began to get ready for the city, for the dormitory in which I live. I went to the dorm because I had a lot of things to do in the city and going from home was inconvenient.

At 3:00 p.m. I went to the training center. We had a thematic lesson. The theme of the lesson was "How to pass a job interview." It was a very interesting lesson, a lot of useful information, especially for me, because in July I plan to get a job where I would have to have an interview. Now I feel much more confident and a little prepared. Diana conducted the lesson; she works in this center.

After the lesson I went to the store and replenished my travel card.

Then, having returned to the dorm, I learned about the graduation at the center. It will be held at the Smart Point, namely at the Amphitheater. I'm very glad.

Then I worked in the kitchen for 3 hours, cooked dinner for tomorrow, and then had dinner with everyone.

Then at 21:00 I took a shower and read a book.

Now I'm going to sleep.

❊ ❊ ❊

*May 18, 2019*

Today I woke up at 8:00 a.m. and took a shower. At 8:30 a.m. I went to breakfast with everyone. At 9:00 a.m. I went to work in the kitchen for 3 hours.

In my dormitory you don't have to pay money, instead you work for 3 hours.

Then at 12:30 p.m. I had lunch. We had fries with steak for lunch, but it was only fries for me, because I don't eat meat.

At 13:30 p.m. I went to buy a book for my sister as a gift for her birthday. I bought *The Adventures of Sherlock Holmes*. She loves detective stories.

Then, at 16:00 p.m., Nellie and I went cycling and bought groceries for an orphanage.

At 17:30 p.m. I went home. I arrived in 1.5 hours.

Mom and I drank delicious green tea with ginger and lemon.

At 20:00 p.m. two of my friends, Aktoty and Aruzhan, came over. We chatted about a lot of things. They left at 21:30 p.m.

*Thank you to the Wonder Foundation and the Kazakhstan Foundation for Cultural, Social and Economic Development for connecting me with Ayaulym.*

# Chanleakna

16 years old

Phnom Penh, Cambodia, and Melbourne, Australia

**What's your favorite thing to do in Phnom Penh?**
Besides studying, I would go out with my grandma and sister or my friends, going to the café or watching movies.

**What are your favorite subjects?**
Currently, I am taking the science-related subjects as well as mathematics and English literature. My favorite subjects right now are chemistry and mathematics.

**Tell us a little about your friends.**
Well, about my friends, I don't really have any. I mean I only have a few true friends who will be there and stick with me through high waves and hard rocks.

**What are your plans for your future, when you grow up?**
I personally want to be a medical scientist but after I graduate Year 12 curriculum here I will take on a Bachelor of Nursing first.

# "It is never easy, leaving your home country and living by yourself at the age of 16. It feels so cold physically and mentally; it feels as if each and every single decision can change your life."

**"I'M JUST AN ORDINARY** 16-year-old girl . . . trying to discover my extraordinary," wrote Leakna in the summer of 2018. She shared diary entries for the "Girlhood Around the World" series that originally appeared in *The Lily*, writing about her days at school, her friends, and her family. At the time, she lived in Phnom Penh, the capital city of Cambodia, which is home to about two million people.[18] The country has one of

the youngest populations in Southeast Asia, with about two-thirds of its people under the age of thirty.[19]

In Phnom Penh, Leakna lived with her grandmother, sister, and aunt. Her parents divorced when she was just two years old, and she hasn't kept in contact with or seen her mother for fourteen years now—"She already has a new family," says Leakna—but she gets along with her dad. Her primary support system,

Phnom Penh,
Cambodia

"emotionally, physically and financially," however, is her grandmother.

In early 2019, when I got back in touch with Leakna for this book, she had moved from Phnom Penh to Australia for school.

"Since forever, I've always wanted to study abroad but I never got the chance to. Now that I got a full accommodation scholarship here in Australia, it was one of the best opportunities I've ever received," she explained.

The process wasn't an easy one: after she was accepted to the school and given a scholarship, Chanleakna had to apply for a visa to be able to live and study in Australia.

Now, Leakna is in Year 11 in Australia (comparable to eleventh grade in the United States), and she's on a rigorous academic path: she wants to become a doctor of medical science. That's what her sister is studying in university, too.

She's got a whole path planned out— Australia offered better opportunities, and she's seizing them with determination. "I decided to move here because I want to be more independent, experience something new, and receive a better education," she explained.

"It's been more than half a year here in Melbourne, Australia, and honestly I sometimes like it and I sometimes don't," says Leakna, "Sometimes I just feel like I made the wrong decision and everything, but it's alright. There are good days and bad days . . . I was homesick most of the time, cried my eyes out."

In these three diary entries, written over the course of nine months and from different continents, Leakna writes both about life before she leaves Phnom Penh and what life looks like across the world and far away from her family. ◊

Melbourne,
Australia

IN CAMBODIA, about 40 percent of girls are in secondary school, or high school.[20]

"In Cambodia's capital, Phnom Penh, many of these girls tell us they feel constrained by social and cultural norms that define what girls can and cannot do, and define what is 'acceptable' for girls," says Kate Heuisler, Chief of Party, United States Agency for International Development (USAID)'s Development Innovations project. She works with young Cambodian women on several programs, including Technovation Cambodia, an all-girl tech entrepreneurship learning program, in which Leakna participated.

"Many families feel strongly that they want girls to pursue certain careers and studies, and many expect their girl children to do all the housework, coordinate family business activities, and stay home in the evenings and on weekends. This is a challenge for any young women that want to explore educational opportunities after school hours," Heuisler says.

But "things are changing across generations and as technology advances," according to Heuisler. More girls have phones and access to the Internet, so they have ways of finding out about opportunities. Even going abroad on a scholarship to study, as Leakna has, is easier for girls now than it was for their older sisters.

Leakna is one of about five million students around the world who travel to another country for education.[21] In fact, there are more than 680,000 international students in Australia, where Leakna now lives and studies.[22] The largest numbers of these students come from China, India, Nepal, Vietnam, and Brazil.[23]

Moving across the world brings great opportunity and also adjustments: learning to navigate a new culture and country, learning to live alone, and learning to live with homesickness, far away from family—all themes Leakna writes about in her diary. ◊

*July 4, 2018*

Hey diary, today is pretty exciting and probably is one of the most satisfying days of this week. So I woke up at 6:30 a.m. and went to school like I normally do but probably with a different excitement. Haha!!! I really can't wait to see the result that will be coming out today evening. Will I be one of the shortlisted candidates that will be selected to go to the next round of the international science competition?* My friend said to me: "Are you going to say hello or are you going to say goodbye to the hectic?" But wait! The result was finally out and it was unexpected, it really was. I was so happy and astonished as well, hehe. I PASSED!!! I AM ONE OF THE SHORTLISTED CANDIDATES, YAYY!

The first thing I did after knowing my result was to call my grandma and daddy telling them that Nana is passing (Nana is my nickname). They were so happy <3. Seeing how delighted they were gave me the courage to continue fighting, I almost teared my eyes out. *shh* aye, I'm tired now. Good night, diary.

✳ ✳ ✳

*July 6, 2018*

So I woke up at 6:30 a.m. when the alarm rang and went to school on time, hehe! What am I really looking forward to today? Hmmm, I

---

* Leakna participated in the Thailand International Science Fair. In 2019, students from sixteen different countries participated in the competition.

hope it won't rain. But expectation went wrong and something that is not supposed to happen, happened. Remember about the shortlisted candidates about the science competition thingy? So the program just suddenly announced that tomorrow is the judge cut-down round. Like wait, what? This is too fast. I can't accept it and they said it is just choosing the topic, going up on stage, and presenting what you are going to do. But hey!!!

Choosing the topic is one of the hardest decisions ever. If you make mistakes about choosing the topic, then sorry. Like oh my god, I talked to their assistant, begged them so hard and they finally agreed to do it another day and extended the deadlines. Phew!!! Thank god, and I went to the café alone and researched about stuff. Well, didn't get to spend my time with friends or family much but mehh! Will do it another day when I'm a little bit more free. Alright another class started at 5:30 p.m. and ended at 7:30 p.m. It's time to go back home . . . get things done and go back to sleep . . . *lights off* goodnight.

✳ ✳ ✳

*April 2019*

I was having a really tough time in Cambodia, I could consider that as a mental breakdown. It feels as if the world is against you and those thoughts keep on running wild in my head. I lost sleep and my appetite. Few weeks have passed, I got my student visa to Australia and it was such a whole new journey for me.

Finally, I can leave all of the unnecessary problems behind and go one step forward. It is never easy, leaving your home country and living by yourself at the age of 16. It feels so cold physically and mentally; it feels as if each and every single decision can change your life. I've learned to be more and more independent and responsive every day.

I mean school is not that bad, I enjoy studying here a lot—just, the subjects and the lessons that I've missed from term 1 are pretty hard to catch up with. Since I skipped one term of the school year, I have to take more subjects than the other students and it is tough. Almost everyone expects and motivates me to do well in school and on the exams. It was such a pressure for me to deal with daily but that's okay, I will do my best. Go to school and come back home . . . I feel really homesick most of the time, I miss my grandmother, dad, sister, and everyone so bad to the point where it tears me down sometimes. But I've made good friends here from Cambodia, China, and the Aussies. I love how people don't judge your choices and no dramas. But yes, being an independent international student is never an easy task but I'll manage to survive anyway. I am so thankful for all the opportunities I'm granted. Forever grateful xX

*Thank you to USAID's Development Innovations project for connecting me with Chanleakna.*

# Chen Xi

## 16
years old

Singapore

### Tell us about your friends.

In my current class, I haven't really made any close friends. I guess I don't really feel like I fit in?

I usually hang out with people from other classes, mostly people I've met through my previous extracurricular (netball) groups and my ex classmates. The ones I'm closest to would be Isabelle, Le Xuan, and Chiao-Yi. I rarely hang out with them now due to our hectic schedules, so thank God for social media.

I have also made many friends in the minuscule yet close-knit humanities community in my school, who I do spend time with frequently as I work together with them often.

I don't really get out of the house, I'm usually at school all day, then I go home and sleep because life is exhausting.

### How do you like to spend your time when you are not at school?

I read, bullet journal, study, watch Netflix, and sleep. I generally read anything that I get my hands on. I'm not sure I have a specific genre I like best.

### What do you watch on TV or Netflix?

I watch LOTS of American TV. I love *Brooklyn Nine-Nine*, *The Good Place*, *Glee*, *Pretty Little Liars*, and *Dynasty*. My all-time favorite is *Elementary*—I maintain that it's the best interpretation of Sherlock Holmes to exist. I also watch French dramas, but that's mainly for the sake of my exams.

# "My favourite subjects are literature and French, even though I do enjoy the other subjects I take. They're really nice reprieves from the sciences."

**CHEN XI LOVES** to read—she'll read anything she can get her hands on—and when I ask her about her dreams for the future, she ends up telling me about *The Great Gatsby* and how "dreams are but mere illusions."

But she also has very practical and specific goals about higher education and what she hopes to study in the future.

"I aspire to read English literature in the UK and hopefully work in academia," she says. "If we're being realistic, however, I would probably major in literature and try to either minor in mathematics or take a second major in the social sciences, most likely psychology. I would attempt to go into education or academia, and I have honestly no idea what I'd do if I failed."

She lives in Singapore with her parents, sister, and grandmother. Her mother is a nurse lecturer and PhD student and her father is a pastor.

Singapore is a very diverse city and home to a lot of immigrants, with a population that's made up primarily of Chinese, Malay, Indian, and other ethnic groups. In fact, about one in five marriages involving Singaporeans are between couples of different races.[24]

Some of this diversity is reflected in Chen Xi's family and education, too. "Neither of my parents has English as a first language," says Chen Xi, who studies, speaks, and writes in English. "Which is odd because I suck at Mandarin (my dad's first language) and I completely don't speak Bahasa Melayu (my mom's I think oops)."

English is one of her favorite subjects, and Chen Xi has also studied Chinese and Malay at school. "I must say though, I've enjoyed every moment of Chinese in secondary school; my teachers have been amazing," she says. "Doesn't make me any less grateful that I'm done with mandatory bilingual education though. We had to take Malay classes, but I used to have dance classes which clashed with the Malay classes in primary [elementary] school."

Chen Xi works hard and spends her days at school and her evenings poring over homework. Sometimes after studying late into the night, she will fall asleep in class the next day. ◊

**SINGAPORE HAS** a reputation for academic rigor and high-achieving students. According to studies of teenage students around the world, students in Singapore top the charts globally in terms of academic excellence.[25] But students in Singapore also reported that academics take a larger emotional toll on them, according to a study conducted in more than 70 countries by the Organization for Economic Cooperation & Development (OECD).

For example, 76 percent of students polled in Singapore reported feeling test anxiety, compared with an average of 55 percent in other OECD countries. Significantly more students from Singapore, when compared to the average, also worried about performing poorly in school.[26]

While Chen Xi is quick to dismiss the stereotype of Asian students who are good at only math and science (she loves French and English literature too), her dedication to academics aligns with the experiences of Singaporean teenagers at large.

"I study because I enjoy it," says Chen Xi. "So yeah, I'm your stereotypical Asian (without the grades, but most of my friends aren't, so please kill that stereotype and let me study because I want to!!). Also I do want to do well so I'll be able to read my subject of choice (which isn't a stereotypical Asian subject of choice thank you very much), in my school of choice." ◊

*Chen Xi often writes in Singaporean slang, and we've included explanations for words you might not be familiar with.*

*March 19, 2019*

Am I writing the year or the day first? I guess we'll never know. Hehe today has been pretty good I guess? Chem was ok and then I ate the UniCornetto it sucks but it's so pretty and I ate the marinara spicy fusilli & it's okay. ok but it was pretty productive! Shalyn and I sat at the café for about an hour doing work & I did some chem & bio & now I'm almost done w the first chapter of bio!! after a month!! two more to go!!!!! also Jaymie's birthday is on thursday so I got her the rose face mask, it's rly good hehe and the shea butter one which I've never tried. and nigel took a photo for us in which I'm probably not looking at the camera let the record show that I'm ugly and embarrassed.

pfft I should go do bio lol the test is on monday take note:

mon: bio test

tues: math test?

weds: chem test

thurs: more probable math test + chem test

or, I could go edit version 3048437 of my campaign poster!! [*] spent half the day on that I don't even know why I signed up but I guess it's a great experience in that it's testing my persistence :)

[*] Chen Xi was running for student council.

*April 2, 2019*

Hi! I'm trying my darndest to keep my handwriting neat after almost failing [a class] bc of my handwriting (you know what I'm gonna fail the test from earlier) and failing french. Gee thanks handwriting! It's been a pretty hectic week and a half. I kinda neglected journaling since 2 saturdays ago so I'm just gonna say that the last day of the hols + Saturday was spent MUGGING [studying] for bio . . . I crammed 3 chapters into my head (bc the test was on Monday) and pulled an all nighter and DIED (okay I pull lots of all nighters, like I'm writing this during an all nighter. Yes I'm running on caffeine).

AND the Bio dept only tested us on organelles and membrane structure?? I studied for carbs bc I was kinda lost and I memorised EVERYTHING and it wasn't even tested :) so that was 2 days wasted, and tbh I don't really remember much else, except that I watched *Victorious* & *Sam and Cat* & *My Little Pony* & *OUAT* in French.

UGH can you see my handwriting getting progressively more disgusting. Okay and as I mentioned, there was French on Weds, I got like 8/30 which isn't bad IF I COULD PASS MATH!! because math was on thursday with chem. For chem, I was failure-bound—okay I just neglected it and I feel so so bad, sorry Mr. W, you're an amazing teacher I'm just dumb/lazy & sorry Mr L I'm just lazy/I prefer artsy [subjects] like french even if I love math <3 My main issue with math is that I have no idea how to use the bloody graphing calculator? I spent more than half the paper tryna work it and just gave up & did it manually & i'm so careless. That's my fatal flaw. So I'm failure-bound for math too wuhu!

Oh and on Saturday, like the Saturday that just ended, we had a basic social! * and yesterday/Monday wasn't very eventful, except for the council rehearsal. †

Anyways, someone commented that I sounded insincere. but idk lol it was cold & I had to sit still and UGH. also Ms. Kai commented that my hair was a mess, well I'm in this constant state of messiness. I AM THE MESS. So today I mugged GP [General Paper, a general-studies class] and the test was weirdly difficult? Maybe I should have slept earlier but I was just so unclear in my writing GOSH the thought of it makes me want to slap myself.

Before I continue, I just remembered on Friday, I fell asleep in Ms. Loh's class. I feel guilty but I was so exhausted, it's been a long week, I just knocked out (I mean not exactly) I was kinda reading articles on genetic innovation, farming opinions, and I just drifted off? and she didn't even scold me, which makes me feel bad, because she's the teacher whom I have respected/actually liked for the longest time in my high school life? and I'm just out here being a disappointment? I have hoped for five years that she'd teach me PW [a subject called

---

* The social was an outing with a group from church. They went to a board game café.
† The rehearsal was for campaign speeches, since Chen Xi was running for student government.

project work] AND I GO AND MESS IT UP BY FALLING ASLEEP?

anyWAYS last week was a bad week which I never want to revisit :(

   So here's the thing, I'm rarely ever bored in lit. If I am, I'm still engaged by the lesson. I absolutely ADORE lit. but for the first time, I sort of zoned out? in class. Which is very out of character for me, as most people would know me as being unable to LIVE without lit! and this was a poetry lesson/I love poetry lessons & analysis! so halfway through the lesson I realized I was dead and was instantly like, 'what's going on smh I need help' and I proceeded to spend the next half an hour resolving to tell Mr. S that I feel like I have reached a plateau in my learning. honestly, I felt super egotistic and bratty and horrid when I told him that. I felt like I have completely stopped learning bc I know you never stop learning for lit, and I feel like a real brat like, 'I'm too good & fast for this class (because he kinda asked me if I felt like the class was less advanced and I said yes and UGH I just feel so bad, it's not that they are not advanced bc they do go through rly deep stuff, it was more of I feel like they are all moving forward, and I'm just standing still. I did clarify this.

   So he kinda offered to give me extra hw, which I will be accepting because homework is the key to solve all problems, and world hunger! at least, fine, poetry analysis and extensive reading and analysis of meter may just do the trick.

# Claudie

13 years old

Pango Village, Vanuatu

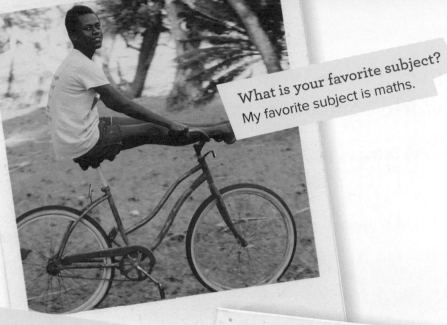

**What is your favorite subject?**
My favorite subject is maths.

**When did you start learning how to surf?**
**What made you decide to learn to surf?**
I started surfing when I was 11 years old. I liked how my sister usually surfs so that made me decided to surf.

**How often do you surf?**
I usually surf on Sundays and sometimes on school days.

# "I want to be Wonder Woman, because whenever the world comes across a big trouble, I would solve it."

**"I WANT TO BE WONDER WOMAN,** because whenever the world comes across a big trouble, I would solve it."

Meet Claudie. She's thirteen, she surfs, and she wants to travel the world. When she grows up, she wants to be a lawyer (as well as Wonder Woman).

She's part of a big family—including six uncles, an aunt, and eighteen cousins—and she lives with her mother, brother, and uncle. They live in a small village in the South Pacific country of Vanuatu, which is made up of a group of about eighty islands and is known for beaches, being the birthplace of bungee jumping, and diving. It routinely ranks as one of the happiest places in the world.[27]

For Claudie, it's also a place where many of her days are spent learning to ride the waves and dreaming about what her grown-up life will look like. In school, math is her favorite subject, and she's worried about her midyear exams. Outside of school and surfing, she likes doing her chores at home, such as washing her clothes and cooking with her mother.

Claudie mostly hangs out with two friends. "I like walking around the village with Genevieve," she says, and, "I like surfing with Salote."

When Claudie was younger, she watched her older sister surf, which inspired her to take up the sport at eleven years old. ◊

Pango Village,
Vanuatu

**GIRLS' SURFING** is a relatively new phenomenon in Vanuatu, as it is in much of the rest of the world. It's part of an effort to help empower women and girls in the region.

"There was a noticeable male dominance in the lineup, which was a reflection of our society's patriarchal culture," explains Stephanie Mahuk, president of the Vanuatu Surfing Association, a local organization that has set up initiatives to empower girls and create surfing opportunities for them. Claudie is part of Solwata Sistas, the program for girls to learn how to surf.

"While the boys believed the surf was their territory and discouraged the girls who tried, most girls themselves believed that medium of ocean enjoyment [surfing] was not for them," Mahuk explains.

The gender inequality in surfing in Vanuatu reflects a patriarchal culture—a culture where men have more authority than women and power over women. It also reflects an inequality between men and women that is widespread in the Pacific Islands. Women have fewer opportunities for jobs, are represented less in government, and sometimes don't share the same rights under the law as men do.

In fact, as of 2018, none of the fifty-two members of Vanuatu's Parliament were women.[28] And about two-thirds of all women in the region are impacted

→

by gender-based violence, which is twice the global average.[29] Gender-based violence includes violence or abuse that is based on someone's gender identity, existing gender norms, or gender-based unequal power relationships. It can include physical violence, sexual abuse, or emotional or psychological abuse.

According to Mahuk, gender roles in Vanuatu still often favor men and give them more opportunities. "[Solwata Sistas] challenges the pervasive sexism and discrimination against girls and women using surfing," she says. "The current climate has become more conducive to bringing about gender parity because other organizations and the government have with louder voices advocated for a change in attitude towards the treatment of girls and women."

As much as girls claiming space on surfboards and in the ocean is about shifting expectations of what girls or women can do with the goal of creating more equality, it is also, of course, about the joy of the sport—of the mental and physical feat of riding a wave.

"A passion for surfing brings about a connection to nature that no other sport does and lands most surfers on the forefront of protecting the environment they enjoy," Mahuk says. ◊

*Friday*

This morning I woke up and went down to the beach and helped to set up tents to sell some Leimalo shirts. *

Then I came home and had my shower and breakfast and went back to the beach to help to set up tents to sell some Leimalo shirts.

Then my friends came over and we hung around the beach. After that it was my heat [to surf] so I jumped into the water.

When I came back I found out that I came in 4th. I felt so unhappy then I cried and my cousin was so mean to me and said something I didn't feel good about and I ran home with my board and cried and cried. I didn't like that day.

✳ ✳ ✳

*Monday*

This morning, I woke up and had breakfast and went down to the beach. Then my cousin told me that my aunt wanted to see me.

When we arrived at my aunt's house, she told me that she wants me to sell her cake. I took the cake and [went] back to the beach. After selling the cake, I went back to my aunt's house and dropped off the container and the money.

Then I hung around the beach, then went back home and told my mum I was sick and she massaged me.

* Leimalo is a local goddess who blesses surfers with good waves.

*Thursday*

Today, I woke up and I felt like I was going to be sick. Then I took my blanket and I slept on the couch. When I woke up I saw my mum folding the blanket and sweeping. After that, she went outside and I had nothing to do, I was just on the couch.

Then I had my breakfast and came back and lay on the couch. I asked my mum if she could buy me credit [pay for more data for her cell phone so she could go online] cause I wanted to go to YouTube.

Then something went wrong with the phone. I tried to find out what's wrong with the phone but I couldn't, so I left the phone on the couch and went to see my cousin.

We were telling stories. After that I came home, had lunch and slept on the couch. Then I remembered that my birthday was on Friday the 26th of April, it was tomorrow. Then I went back to sleep.

✳ ✳ ✳

*Sunday*

Today I woke up, I folded my blanket and left it on my bed and went to the kitchen to have breakfast.

After that I asked my mum if I can go to my uncle's house to use his wifi. Then she said yes, then I took the phone and went [to my uncle's house where I used] the wifi [to] watch some movies. Then I had lunch. After that I decided to go to my other uncle's house, so I went and watched a movie on their laptop. Then the sun was about to go down, then I came back home.

When I reached the house I looked for my mum but she wasn't here so I thought she went to my grandmother's house. So I went there . . .

She wasn't there so I came back. When I was walking back, I saw them walking back home from the garden so I followed them back, had my shower and dinner, and went to bed at 8 o'clock.

*Thank you to Vanuatu Surfing Association for connecting me with Claudie.*

# Desireé

## 15
### years old

Dubai, United Arab Emirates

### Tell us about your friends.
I guess you could say that I do have a lot of friends, but recently my really close friends and I have been drifting apart—mostly because of school and studying and prepping for boards, so we aren't as close anymore. Lately I've been making new friends though, so I'm starting to become really close with them. They are all really nice and I feel like I fit in with them.

### What are your favorite subjects in school?
Probably history and geography. Maybe even business.

### Do you have a best friend?
My best friend is Neeraj. We go to the same school and we have for years, but we became really good friends at a Justin Bieber concert in 2017. Neeraj is really fun to hang out with and he's extremely smart! He's always been there for me and I hope we remain friends forever!!

"I guess you could say that I do have a lot of friends, but recently my really close friends and I have been drifting apart—mostly because of school and studying and prepping for boards, so we aren't as close anymore."

**DESIREÉ LIVES IN DUBAI** with her mom, her mother's husband, and her dog, Pixie. Her parents are divorced, and her father lives nearby.

Dubai, a city in the Middle East, is known for its glittering skyscrapers (it is home to the Burj Khalifa, the world's tallest building) and its diverse population.

The life Desireé describes in this big city includes going to events and studying hard. When she's not at school or doing her homework, she likes spending time with friends going to concerts and the mall, or staying home with her dog.

"I have a large family," she says. "But not many live nearby. The majority of my family stays in India and the rest in Canada and Australia." Desireé's immediate family migrated from India to the United Arab Emirates, or UAE, for work. ◊

Dubai,
United Arab Emirates

**DESIREÉ'S FAMILY** is part of a large migrant population in Dubai and the UAE. People from all over the world come to Dubai for jobs—more than 90 percent of the population is non-Emirati.[30] A significant percentage of these migrants or expats come from South Asian countries such as India, Pakistan, and Bangladesh. Some come to Dubai as office workers, with jobs in finance or oil and gas companies, while others come to work as construction workers, drivers, or housemaids.[31]

For many of the people who come to Dubai from other countries, life can be difficult: reports from the city regularly document exploitation of migrant workers, many of whom have faced forced labor, horrific working conditions, and assault.[32] ◊

*Tuesday, February 12, 2019*

The weather was amazing today! Before going to school I checked the weather forecast and it said it was going to rain a lot. So I was hoping for a half day at school. It ended up raining a lot, but we had a full day of school. It even rained during break! Aida, Minnah, and I were standing in the rain during break. After school Nazneem came home. She was helping me with my dance for PE. We changed the song I was dancing to. I was really tired by the end of the day, so I didn't do much in the evening. After Nazneem left, I studied a little and that was it.

✳ ✳ ✳

*Thursday, February 14, 2019*

Today is Valentine's Day & RedFest. We had a secret valentine at school today. I got Anaina, so I bought her this cute heart-shaped chocolate box and put it in a cute bag. And Aida was my secret valentine. She got me a really cute candle and a unicorn pen. After school I came home and started getting ready for RedFest. RedFest is basically a concert with around 4 artists that perform on each day. There are 2 days. I went for day 1. It was amazing. Even though we had to wait in line forever. It was so hyped and amazing!

*Friday, February 15, 2019*

After RedFest yesterday I was too tired to go for the Walk for Education* in the morning. I just could not wake up. I studied some geography today. Today has been a pretty low day. I was home alone a lot, but I did study in that time which was good, but no still it was a pretty boring low-key day. I didn't sleep until after 12 a.m. I was lazing around and watching TV after studying. My doggy, Pixie, and I cuddled a lot today! It was nice.

Desireé <3

PS: I also have my PE Board Exam[†] recording on Sunday and I'm super stressed and worried about how things will go.

* The Walk for Education is an annual walk hosted by a philanthropic organization in Dubai.

[†] Desireé was preparing to take the International General Certificate of Secondary Education exams. These are standardized tests across many subjects, including physical education, or PE.

# Diza

## 14
### years old

Mumbai, India

**How do you like to spend your time when you are not at school?**

I love singing and recording my voice while I do so, I like going out with my friends, and I love spending time with my twin sister, who is my number one best friend!

**What are your favorite subjects in school?**

Physics, music, and English

**What do you want to do when you grow up? What are your dreams?**

I have always enjoyed singing and would love to pursue it as a hobby, and I'm still deciding if I want to make it a career. If not, I enjoy fashion designing as well.

"As a girl, especially, the words *cool* and *cute* have literally become a definition. The ones who don't fit into these so-called definitions are not noticed as much as the ones who do, regardless of their inner beauty."

**DIZA LIVES IN** a high-rise building with a view of Mumbai's glittering skyline. In a room she shares with her twin sister, Diza does homework, plays the guitar, sings, and chats with friends.

But Diza hasn't always lived in Mumbai. Her family has moved time and time again for her father's job, so she has grown up in cities across the world—in Singapore, Cape Town, New Delhi, and now Mumbai.

"When I was younger, I hated the idea of shifting all the time because of my dad's jobs," says Diza. "Now, I'm so glad we did. I have friends from different parts of the world, I got to learn various cultures and certainly got a lot of exposure."

Since Diza has moved so many times—to different cities and different schools—she has had to navigate

Mumbai,
India

belonging, fitting in, and finding and making friends many times. Her perspective is different from those of girls who have grown up in one place.

When she was writing her diary entries, Diza was thinking a lot about the expectations girls face—to be "cool" and "cute," to belong to the right cliques, to be popular. These concerns are nearly universal—whether you're watching *Mean Girls* or you live in Mumbai or Montreal. But according to academics who study teenage friendship, close friends are better for us than popularity.

"My research showed that teens who had closer friendships during middle adolescence had decreased depression and anxiety in early adulthood, while teens who were more focused on popularity actually had higher social anxiety as young adults," explains Rachel Narr, an academic at the University of Virginia. "So, it seems that although popularity affords some short-term benefits, it's deeper, closer friendship that likely confers positive benefits over time." ◊

**ONE DAY,** a few weeks after sharing her diary entries, Diza sent me photos on WhatsApp from a poor neighborhood near her house. With narrow and winding streets and small houses cramped close together, it looked vastly different from the world where Diza lived. She explained she was visiting this part of the city because she was curious about the neighborhood, and her trip highlighted the widespread economic disparity in Mumbai and India.

In a country of more than a billion people, it's hardly surprising that there are many different types of living circumstances. But economic inequality in India is stark: the richest 10 percent of Indians own more than three-quarters of the entire country's wealth.[33]

Mumbai, which is India's financial capital, is home to more than 50,000 millionaires and 28 billionaires.[34] At the same time, more than 40 percent of the city's population live in slums,[35] like the one Diza visited. These are neighborhoods where the poorest people live in homes that might not have solid foundations or walls, and in conditions that are often overcrowded and lacking in formal sanitation. ◊

*April 1, 2019*

Dear Diary,

Today has been super miserable, but at the same time exciting. Miserable because our incredible and memorable trip to Denmark, Norway, and Sweden has officially ended. However, I am extremely excited to see my friends again at school. Moreover, it's my first day in Grade 10 tomorrow! There are definitely emotions. Nevertheless, I am up for whatever comes my way this year. It's thrilling. In the past 2 weeks, I have spent a lot of quality time with my dear family. I am the happiest person in the world when travelling around this fascinating, diverse world, especially with my amazing family.

Right now, I'm thinking how my life would be after I graduate and study in a place away from my parents, about 3 years from now.

Life will come with its challenges but I'll have to find every possible way to conquer them. Again, it's scary, but at the same time, I'm really looking forward to doing what I love and experimenting with things throughout life. Today, I've learnt that all good things must come to an end. This vacation was one of the best things in my life. However, it couldn't last forever. Besides, there are lots more upcoming happy times yet to live.

<3 Today's quote: <3

"All life is experiment. The more experiments you make, the better"

*April 2, 2019*

As a girl, especially, the words *cool* and *cute* have literally become a definition. It's heard by me every single day at school. The ones who don't "fit" into these so-called definitions are not noticed as much as the ones who do, regardless of their inner beauty. I feel as though in this generation, MOST people don't even bother considering what's on the inside.

It feels as though the quote "don't judge a book by its cover" has suddenly disappeared. Today, I also realized at school that sticking by your truest & best friends is all you need to do. The ones who are mean don't matter. All they want is to see you being unhappy. We need to focus on what's important and that is it.

"The ones who talk behind your back are behind you for a reason."

I have learnt to surround myself with the people I love. The people who support me & understand me for who I am. They find their happiness in mine. And with them, I'm the happiest person in the world.

✳ ✳ ✳

*April 3, 2019*

Dear Diary,

It's currently 8 p.m. Today, nothing special really happened. I want to tell you something that happened at school though. It was really nasty to see, to be honest.

My sister and I are friends with some people who aren't popular and barely have any friends at school. Today, we dropped them back home. Other friends of ours saw this and they gave us dirty looks. This happens whenever I hang out with people who aren't so "cool" and "popular."

However, I still love them as my friends and no matter what others say, I always want to be friends with them. Anyway, when I got back from school, after a few hours, I had my singing class. This is my "stress relief." Whenever I sing, all troubles suddenly vanish. It makes me sooo happy. <3 Right now I'm just waiting for dinner. Another night spent with my incredible family! <3

I decided today's quote to be this one by Eunice Camacho Infante: "In the end, people will judge you anyway. Don't live your life impressing others, live your life impressing yourself."

# Emilly

## 18
years old

São Paolo, Brazil

**What are your favorite subjects?**
My favorite subjects are chemistry, and I like math a lot, even though it's the subject I find the hardest.

**Who do you live with?**
My daughter and my husband

**Can you tell us about your parents?**
My mom is sick; she doesn't work. My dad is a driver, but I don't talk to him or have affection for him.

**Tell us a little about your friends.**
Now, I am a more reserved person, I don't have a lot of friends, I always like to be by my family's side, every time we can. I stopped drinking, hanging out . . . I am a more chill person today!

"I do get a little sad because I didn't ask to be born and go through all that, but I am proud of the person I am today and all of this influences the way I mother!"

**WHEN I ASKED EMILLY** about herself, she shared a list of dreams. Here, in her own words, is her list:

1. To become a doctor.
2. To have a lot of money and open a lot of nonprofit organizations to help the people that need help!
3. To give the whole world to my daughter!
4. To make my YouTube channel bigger!

Emilly is eighteen and lives in São Paulo with her baby daughter, Sofia, and her husband. She grew up in a favela—one of the city neighborhoods that are sometimes called slums or shantytowns. They are crowded with small houses, sometimes made of tin or cardboard.[36] Not all favelas are the same—while some have homes with phone lines and computers,[37] many don't have formal toilets or access to water or electricity. About 1.5 million people in São Paolo live in favelas.[38]

São Paolo,
Brazil

Growing up in poverty and facing abuse, Emilly has had to handle a lot of hardship, and achieving her dreams will mean overcoming more obstacles, such as finding a way to get childcare support and to pay for college.

But she has many plans for the future, both for herself and for her baby girl. Her biggest dream, she says, is to become a doctor. She wants the same for her daughter, too.

"I am 18 years old and I thought about giving up so many times, especially because it's such a long, hard tough way," she says. "And I don't have money to go to college and become the woman I dream of! But I still have a lot of faith and determination that one day I will get there! I believe doors will open eventually and I will conquer the whole world." ◊

THERE ARE HUNDREDS of thousands of young mothers like Emilly in Brazil, and nearly one in five babies born in Brazil are born to teenage mothers, according to Brazil's Ministry of Health.[39]

Emilly is not in school at the moment, but she's eager to continue her education and she is planning to take a national exam this year to earn a high school diploma.

About three-quarters of all teenagers with children in Brazil, like Emilly, have dropped out of school. Caring for a baby takes priority over attending classes to finish their education, limiting both their educational attainment and their opportunities for jobs.[40]

Teenage pregnancy can also be dangerous for both the mother's health and the baby's health. Medical complications related to pregnancy and childbirth are the leading cause of death for fifteen- to nineteen-year-old girls around the world.[41] ◊

79

*Translated from Portuguese*

I am going to talk a little bit about my life. It was a little hard, but I choose to talk about it because I imagine there are a lot, of other girls that suffered like me in a community somewhere. I am not talking about a regular community; I am talking about favelas! People running from left to right! I was born and raised in one of those.

My mom has some mental problems, problems she manages to deal with! But she is still sick . . . And didn't manage to take good care of me in my childhood! She was abandoned after getting pregnant by my father! She didn't have a family to support her or a structure to take care of her and myself! She didn't have money, nothing! But even though she decided not to abort me! And I am extremely grateful for her to have endured so much pain!

I was raised by myself, taking care of myself ever since I was little. At 4 I suffered my first sexual harassment by my mom's boyfriend! She didn't believe though! After that I went to live with my aunt! I used to sleep by her foot, but I am grateful to have a roof over my head! I begged a lot for money on the streets during my childhood and suffered a lot of sexual abuses! I had depression, and every day I would eat in a different house. Maybe you are reading this now and might be imagining that I am crying while I write about my history, but no, I am not! I am happy to have gone through all of this and for being this person that I am today!

I do get a little sad because I didn't ask to be born and go through all that, but I am proud of the person I am today and all of this influences the way I mother today! A mother that will never allow my daughter to suffer not even 1% all I have been through.

Despite all these things, I am well today, because I had to stay well! My faith in Jesus made me believe that everything I have gone through is now past! And that he had written something new for me!

Believing in all that, I managed to overcome all my fears! Today I am 18 years old, I am married, I have a house, a family that loves me a lot, and a beautiful Jesus!

✳ ✳ ✳

A lot of the time during my pregnancy I thought I wouldn't be capable of taking care of my daughter, because people would put pressure on me! I couldn't believe I would be able to educate her, love her, take care of her the way she needed! I thought I wouldn't be able to buy all the things she would need during her life!

But then she was born! And I did it! Because I believed I was capable! Of course I was scared but did it anyways! (Laughs)

Then, she was born! She is a cute little girl! So dependent on me!

And I can manage, I learnt everything is a question about being able to control our emotional and our psychological health, and everything will work out.

✳ ✳ ✳

After she was born, our house got better, the environment got better, she had all the attention, and all of our day is dedicated to her! We have to bathe her, feed her, put her to sleep, change diapers all the time! She makes my bed dirty almost every day, when we take her diaper out, especially during the night, it's so complicated! I am usually exhausted at those times, and this is exactly the time she has to throw a party at the house! She is awake all night, and she is only 17 days old!

But the love we feel for her makes our energy refill so fast that we don't even know where it comes from, but we manage to provide for her. Our days with her are incredible! Me and her dad have a lot of plans! We want to travel, visit places, study, do so many things!

# Emma

16
years old

A Small Village by the Sea, Ireland

### What are your favorite subjects?

English is one of my favorite subjects except I wish we did a lot more on English literature and poetry—especially poetry! I don't know why but after studying for the junior cycle English exam last year (a serious exam everyone in secondary school in Ireland takes), I've started to really enjoy poems and the meanings behind them. I love the meanings behind Robert Frost's poems—they're so powerful.

WHEN YOU
MISS ME
CLOSE YOUR
EYES

SHAWN MENDES
THE TOUR

### Tell us about your dog.

I have a very hyper dog who happens to be called Sonic. He is so crazy and unpredictable that in ways he is like the little brother I never had. I do love him, though, don't get me wrong!

### What do you want to do when you grow up?

I'm not too sure—the ultimate dream is to become a published author. In ways though I think it might just be a faraway fantasy that won't ever happen. Either because I don't have the belief in myself or it just appears impossible to get a job like that in the industry, but who knows? I have determination when I put my mind to it.

# "My whole life revolves around music. I can't imagine my world without it."

**EMMA IS A** sixteen-year-old girl who lives in Ireland with her parents and her dog. She is in her transition year in school, an optional year in secondary school (or high school) that isn't focused entirely on academics, giving teens a chance to widen their horizons by trying new activities and going on trips.

Most of Emma's days consist of school—she loves English and history and wants to continue studying them in college—spending time with friends and family, and listening to music. She writes a lot about music and the pop stars she loves. Her favorite is Shawn Mendes, a Canadian singer.

"I love Shawn Mendes so much because his music has helped me in so many ways," Emma explains. "I think it's nice how he's not that much older than me, so he has a lot of really powerful songs that I can connect to as we're going through the same things at the same time, such as anxiety and growing up."

Emma's walls are plastered with posters and photos of Shawn and other musicians she adores. She also runs Instagram and Twitter fan accounts for Shawn Mendes, which is one of her favorite hobbies. She follows news about him, watches livestreams from around the world, and talks to other fans.

"I've made some really great friends through the fan account from countries such as Belgium and England," she said. "I haven't met up with any of them in person yet but next time Shawn tours around Europe I'm planning to meet up with them." ◊

**ACCORDING TO EXPERTS,** being a superfan like Emma can be an important and transformative experience.

"For teenage female fans, fandom may provide a space for exploring identity, sexuality, creativity, and ambition," explains Dr. Ruth Deller, an academic at Sheffield Hallam University who studies gender and fandom. She says that these communities of fans "are 'safer' [spaces] than at school or home."

"In 'real life' teenage girls often feel disempowered and as though their voices are not taken seriously. In fandoms, there is more of a sense of an even playing field," Deller explains.

For Emma, it's also a space where other people share her interest and don't get bored with her talking about Shawn.

"The fan account is my go-to place where I can talk about Shawn 24/7 and no one can tell me to stop!! My parents and friends from school are sick of me talking about him at this stage!!" she explains.

From the Beatles in the 1960s to Justin Bieber in recent years, the world of pop music fandom is one where "girls' tastes dominate and are praised," according to Dr. Francesca Coppa, a professor

at Muhlenberg College who has studied pop culture, fans, and social media.

This is particularly valuable, Coppa says, in part because "it's a rarer and more valuable experience precisely to the extent to which teenage girls often are not listened to, do not have their taste, art, or writing appreciated."

The communities for devoted fans like Emma are a space where girls find each other, and where their voices and preferences are loud, respected, and heard. For girls around the world, opportunities for this are still too rare. ◊

*March 24*

Today was a really good day. I woke up this morning at around 9:00 a.m. (yes—I know—extremely early, for a night owl like me). I checked my messages on my phone before I got out of bed—the usual. Then, I see in my Instagram feed that while I was asleep . . . Jack Gilinsky from Jack & Jack [an American pop music duo] had liked 2 of my posts on my fanpage for them. I was in shock. Johnson [the other Jack in Jack & Jack] had only noticed me a few days previously for the first time too.

My whole life revolves around music. I can't imagine my world without it. Shawn Mendes, Jack & Jack, and Ariana Grande would be who I mainly listen to. I'm basically borderline obsessed with Shawn and anyone who knows me could tell you that. I have over 40 pictures of him on my bedroom wall. I run another fan account online about Shawn with over a thousand followers. I sleep, breathe, and eat his music. It's so incredible to think that he is only 20—4 years older than me—and has done so much already. "In My Blood" was the song that pushed me through the two grueling weeks of the junior cert* last year. Ariana is such a role model I feel to me and other teenage girls. She shows us anything is possible and she defies all rules. One of my best friends Alicya and I really want to see her live this year when she comes on tour to Dublin and scream out the lyrics to "thank u, next," as it has a special meaning to us, but the tickets are too expensive—300 euro! (I'd only pay that price for Shawn . . .)

My parents and I went to mass as usual today, as it is Sunday. We went to an 11:00 a.m. mass today which is a surprise as we're usually too

* Junior cert, or junior certificate, consists of government-mandated exams in a wide range of subjects that students in Ireland generally take when they're fourteen or fifteen years old.

lazy to get up that early and go for a 5:30 p.m. mass instead and get takeaway after. I wouldn't say I'm an extremely religious person but I do find peace in prayer. After, I went out with my friend Holly. We only live across the road from each other and I've known her for so long—the years are countless. We went to the pavilions and discussed all things Shawn Mendes (what else, of course). We're seeing him live in concert in 19 days too! I can't believe it, it's getting so so close. I remember last year looking at the days away and it was 230 days! We found some Shawn Mendes t-shirts in H&M to our delight and we had McDonald's to finish off the day. I can never say no to a Big Mac!

Emma

✳  ✳  ✳

*April 3*

Dear Diary,

It's so weird how possibly one of the worst days of your life can be followed by one of the best days of your life. Last weekend, I was eating my breakfast in the kitchen and all of a sudden I heard the intro of "In My Blood" playing on the radio. I was delighted because in my opinion, the Irish radio stations never play enough of Shawn's music. However, "In My Blood" quickly turned into the beat of "Treat You Better," and then a voiceover came on the radio about a meet-and-greet competition—to meet—MEET—Shawn Mendes. Both my dad and Sonic were in the kitchen at the time and they both looked at me very alarmed when I started screaming and jumping up and down like a 5-year-old. I straight away started contacting the radio station in every way possible. I set up a Facebook account to specifically spam their comments page, I tweeted them, I emailed them, and also on Instagram through my Shawn Mendes fan account.

Monday was the first day of the weeklong competition. They were giving away the tickets just after I finished school at 4; I used both of my parents' phones to increase my chances along with my own phone. We were told to text in as soon as a song by Shawn Mendes was played; within the first second of the song I texted in. The first person the DJ tried to contact live on the radio, phone went straight to voicemail. So, the second caller won the tickets. Meanwhile, I got a message on my phone saying "missed call." I rang the caller back quick and I heard a voiceover speaking: it was then that I realised I was the first caller, but my phone went straight to voicemail and I would have been meeting my idol if my phone had been working.

I cried hysterically for 2 hours straight after that. I love Shawn more than anything and as I said in another diary entry, my life revolves around his music. So there's nothing I would want more than to thank him for his music as it has helped me through so much. I tried to be positive the next day at school but to be honest, I hadn't got any sleep, I had a fake smile plastered across my face and little did people know there was tears behind my eyes. Not many people understand how much Shawn means to me except a few—Alicya was really helpful. She's also obsessed with

Ed Sheeran so she just put herself in my shoes and understood how I felt straight away. My mum was also really comforting when I came home from school at lunchtime (I always come home for lunch as I only live about 5 mins away from school).

I heard on the radio station at lunchtime that they were giving away more meet and greet tickets during the afternoon. My hands were shaking and my heart started beating at triple speed. I didn't have much hope to win the competition anymore but I knew I still had to try or well, that's what all the YouTube videos I had watched told me to do. I took the afternoon off school and entered the competition. It seemed pretty difficult at first. We were told to form a correct word from a mashup of three Shawn Mendes songs. We had to take the first letter of each song to form a 3-letter word. However, I got it without any hesitation. I sent the answer in and about a minute later, my mum's phone started flashing! I answered it eagerly—a lady introduced herself from the radio show. She told me that my answer was correct and that if the DJ whose name was Tony called my name out—I had to scream as loud as I could as there were a few other callers on the line who could be picked. To my shock, she called out my name and said the words that I dreamed of so many times: "Emma, you're going to meet Shawn Mendes."!!!

I started screaming and freaking out—I was nearly in tears. I couldn't believe that after everything that had happened the day before—I was picked again. Now I can say I'm meeting Shawn in 10 days. It's definitely amazing to see what a new day can bring!

Emma

*Thank you to Fighting Words Ireland for connecting me with Emma.*

# Favour

## 13
### years old

Minna, Nigeria

**Tell us about your friends.**

Their names are Deborah, Comfort, Helene, Cynthia, and so on. I like to spend time with them at school. We read together, we study together, we do everything together. When I'm moody, they make me smile.

**How do you like to spend time when you're not at school?**

I like to spend time with my cousin-sister. Her name is Mercy. We joke around, we talk.

**What are your favorite subjects?**

I will have to make chemistry, biology, mathematics, and English as my favorite subjects, mostly biology.

# "I hate to see or hear that someone died as a result of giving birth . . . that is what gave me the courage to [want to] be a medical doctor."

**"MY DREAM IS** to become a qualified medical doctor," says Favour, "because I want to save people's lives."

Favour lives in Minna, in Niger State, with her parents and her two younger brothers. "I love my area because it is always busy, it doesn't make someone feel bored but rather lively," she says. Her mother is a teacher and her father is in the military, and her dream is to become a surgeon, focusing on maternal medicine.

"I hate to see or hear that someone died as a result of giving birth . . . that is what gave me the courage to [want to] be a medical doctor," she explains.

Favour is a determined science student—she even writes that she'll have

to make biology her favorite subject since she wants to become a doctor. Her parents have encouraged her education. "I love my parents so much because they care for me, they also raise some money to send me and my siblings to school," she says.

Unlike Favour, however, many girls in Nigeria are not in school. In July 2017, Nigeria's government said that the country had "the largest number of children out of school" in the world. Most of them are in the North East of Nigeria, whereas Favour lives in Central Nigeria.[42] According to UNICEF, an estimated 10.5 million Nigerian children, 60 percent of them girls, are not in school.[43] ◊

Minna,
Nigeria

**THE NIGERIA WE SEE** through Favour's eyes is very different from the one that has made headlines in the last decade. Boko Haram, a powerful extremist group, has brought violence, limited women's and girls' rights, closed schools, and displaced hundreds of thousands of Nigerians, among other horrors. They are particularly active in the North East of the country.

The group's name, Boko Haram, translates from Hausa, a widely spoken language in northern Nigeria, to "Western education is forbidden." The group has targeted schools, teachers, and students.[44]

In 2014, 276 schoolgirls were kidnapped from Chibok, a town in northern Nigeria. This incident made international headlines and inspired a trending hashtag (#BringBackOurGirls) as the world watched in horror.[45]

In 2017, a large number of the Chibok girls returned home, but the insurgency continues in parts of the country.[46] According to the United Nations, between 2013 and 2018, more than one thousand children in northeastern Nigeria were abducted by Boko Haram,[47] and more than one thousand schools were destroyed. In February 2018, more than one hundred schoolgirls were kidnapped by Boko Haram in one day.[48] ◊

*Tuesday*

On Tuesday morning when I woke up, I prayed, thanking God for sparing my life, and then later on I did my house chores and then we ate our breakfast and then prepared to go to church. Before then my dad who just arrived from his work came back with gifts for us and we were very happy.

My day was interesting, because we were expecting our dad to come back and our expectations came through. My day was also a good day because I had time to jest with my dad, who I had not seen for weeks.

I woke up today at 5:30 a.m. because of my mum who woke me to help her to feed my junior brother and at the same day I went to bed at about 8:30 p.m. because I was very tired. I am very happy today because I spent time with my family and also with my friends.

I am most looking forward to night coming so that I can rest my brain and sleep.

⁂

*Wednesday*

On Wednesday morning I woke up at about 6:30 a.m. When I woke up I prayed as usual and then greeted my parents, and then went to the kitchen to cook for my brothers because they were hungry, and then

I fetched water and then washed plates. I didn't do all my house chores because I was not feeling too well.

My day today was not that good because I was not feeling too well and my body was weak and because of that I went to the hospital for a checkup and then the doctor prescribed some drugs for me and I took them.

Today I am most looking forward to night coming and then for me to get well and okay soon. I went to bed today at about 7:45 p.m. because I was not feeling too well.

✳ ✳ ✳

*Thursday*

Oh my day. Thursday was a very interesting day for me because my expectations came true. I woke up today at about 6:50 a.m., I prayed, I greeted my parents, did my house chores because I am fit and well today.

My day today was bad because we heard news that one of our relatives was dead. She died as a result of sickness. We were not happy the way we used to be happy because she is very close to us. My mum and her friend went to greet them while we stayed back at home with our last born, who is still a baby so we had to stay back and take good care of the baby.

Moreover, on this very day, I met my uncle who works in another state as a military man; he came to visit us. And my happier thing was that he did not come empty handed. He bought some goodies for us, which we ate like never before.

I really enjoy my day today because I spent time with my uncle. I am most worried today about the issue of my relative who died as a result of ill health. [I wish] I had the capacity to take care of her family and her children.

*Thank you to WAAW Foundation and their fellows for connecting me with Favour.*

# Halima

## 17
### years old

Mazar-i-Sharif, Afghanistan

**What are your favorite subjects in school?**
Quran, biology, geology, and English

**What music do you like?**
Celine Dion

**Tell us about your friends.**
Coming to my relations with friends, indeed I do not have that many friends, as I have realized that it is difficult to trust people. So far, I have made six friends in my life that I really want them to be with me and I want to know them more. All my six friends are school students and they love to go sightseeing.

"Every time a male wins the competition and not a female. However, I never give up. That is why I participate again and again in these competitions."

**WHAT IS IT LIKE** to grow up in a country that is ranked as one of the worst places in the world to be a woman? To grow up in a country at war?

Halima lives with her family in a city in northern Afghanistan. She shared diary entries from the summer of 2018 and early 2019.

For Halima, the days start early— usually around 4 a.m.—and are full: she goes to school, does her chores, helps her father peel potatoes (he sells fries), and teaches English at an academic center. She's hardworking, ambitious, and has big dreams. "I would like to finish my education and become self-sufficient and independent as well as financially support my family," she explains.

While Halima's ambition is echoed by many girls, she faces an additional challenge of living in a country where women's rights have been severely

Mazar-i-Sharif,
Afghanistan

limited and which is ranked as one of the worst in the world for girls' access to education.[49]

From 1996 to 2001, Afghanistan was ruled by the Taliban, an extreme Islamic group. During their reign, women and girls were not allowed to work, go to school, show skin in public, or leave the house without a male family member who would be a "chaperone."[50]

Since then, laws and attitudes have been changing. Now, more than seventeen years after the fall of the Taliban, girls are going to school. "The public space, the public arena, for girls ebbs and flows with these dynamics," as do safety and security in the region, explains Ginna Brelsford, executive director of Sahar, an organization working to get girls into school and keep them there. "There's just enough time that's gone by since 2001, dads and brothers and male figures can weigh out the pros and cons of their daughters going to school, and it keeps tipping more towards education and opportunity, away from the burqa and toward education," she says. ◊

**SINCE 2001,** Afghanistan has been engaged in a conflict—fighting between the Taliban, which no longer controls the government, and the United States, Afghan troops, and international allies—and it has impacted safety and access to schools. All in all, the ongoing conflict resulted in the closing of more than 1,000 of Afghanistan's 17,500 schools.[51]

This has kept a lot of children out of school. Different sources, such as the government and human rights organizations, have different estimates, but according to data from 2016, about 40 percent of all school-aged children in Afghanistan do not attend school.[52] And of the 3.5 million children who are not in school, a staggering 85 percent are girls.[53]

The future of the ongoing conflict, politics, and girls' and women's rights remain uncertain in Afghanistan.

"When you've been at war for decades, there's a way of navigating life, it's a little bit of, 'if god wills.' You know, that phrase is used all the time," says Brelsford. "I think you live in the present in a very significant way because you don't know what's going to happen tomorrow."

In addition to security concerns, gender norms and expectations also play a part in keeping girls out of school.

"Afghan society is still men dominating society," Halima says. "People do not believe in the power of their daughters. They think that only boys can do anything." She also mentions that she was born in Daikundi, another province of Afghanistan, where child marriage is common and can keep girls from pursuing education. "In Daikundi, usually families marry off their daughters in a very young age and do not let them to go to school," she says. "I am very thankful for being in Mazar-i-Sharif. This way I can continue my education." She has continued her education both in school and at religious centers.

Girls here are legally allowed to marry at 16 (or 15, if her father or a judge allows it). About one-third of girls in Afghanistan are married before they turn 18 and, once married, are made to drop out of school.[54]

It is still not the norm for a teen-age girl to go to school, to speak out about her life in public spaces, or to want to enter the professional sphere as Halima does. It could even be seen as a political act, or an act of resistance, since girls are traditionally seen only as daughters, wives, and mothers, not equals to men.

But Halima, and girls like her, are slowly trying to turn the tide in Afghanistan. ◊

*Translated from Dari. Halima shared diary entries from summer 2018 for the series in The Lily—excerpts of those are included, along with entries from spring 2019.*

*Summer 2018*

Every morning, I wake up at 4 a.m. I pray, read some Quran, and then do my homework. After this, I do some chores around the house. I usually finish at 7 a.m. and go to school. I spend four hours in school and come back home and then do my homework. Then, I clean the rooms, wash the dishes from lunch, and then go to Quran school.

In addition to the above work, I also peel potatoes, because my dad sells fries. We usually help him out at home.

I did a lot of work today. First of all, I did home chores. Then reviewed my school lessons and also for leisure I read some books. I wrote some English essays too. Then I headed to school and studied some more. When I got off from school, I did assignments. It was time for collective prayers, after which follows a talk. I thought about it for a while then headed to tutoring classes, studied for one hour then taught for another. I always fight problems, never give up and do my work as best as I can.

I started my day with excitement because I participated in a religious competition.* I have participated in many competitions but have not won or got any sort of prizes. Every time a male wins the competition and not a female.

However, I never give up. That is why I participate again and again in these competitions. I repeat to myself, "If men can win; we can too." Finally, last week I won second prize in a competition that I participated in at school. That is why my day went great!

* This competition was held on the day honoring Bibi Fatima Zahra's birthday. She was the daughter of the Holy Prophet Mohammad in Islam. The day is also called Mother's Day.

*Spring 2019*

By God's blessings, I start my days by praying and reciting holy Quran. After serving my breakfast I prepare for my teaching classes—I teach English for two or three hours in separate classes at an academic center. When the classes are over I return home and it's lunchtime. After having lunch, I wash dishes and go straight to my room in order to study and get prepared for the next day. I mostly study books in the English language, interpret English songs, topics, and sentences. Because I believe that only by making efforts and being curious can I reach my goals. I usually spend my days with laughter and joy; when I go to my class and teach people who are older than me, I feel more confident. It is also worth mentioning that when I see my family and friends happy, I feel more relaxed.

Currently, schools are not active as we are in winter vacations. Schools will resume after a month, and I impatiently count the days approaching to the start of school.

By the way, life has its ups and downs. Some days are passed sadly but some days are passed happily. Today, I was happy as it was Mother's Day. I congratulated my mom on her day and held a small family party on the occasion of Mother's Day. And also, there was a gathering held by the training center where more than 200 people participated, including people's representatives [government officials]. I was happy to be one of the participants at the gathering, as such gatherings are good for increasing our knowledge and awareness regarding our cultures and customs. Such gatherings help us to become more familiar with our national customs and how to follow them properly. Generally, it was a good day for me.

I wish to become self-sufficient and serve my nation along with my brothers. How long should we be victims of traditional society? Women are not only for staying at home and doing housework, but they have capability and they are able to work as men and become financially independent. We Afghan women should not follow Western culture, but we should carry on following our Islam religion and wearing hijab, so that nobody would be able to criticize us.

I have many plans and I really want to fulfill them. After graduating from school, I would like to apply for the institute of midwifery and become a successful midwife, as well as get the chance to enter university as an English lecturer. If I failed to do so (become a lecturer), I will choose journalism. As a journalist I would like to serve my nation and raise their voice. I really want to promote women's awareness regarding their rights as they should become aware of their human and legal rights.

I am concerned about the current situation of Afghanistan. In particular, the condition of women worries me more than any other thing, as people are still not aware of women's rights and most families do not allow their daughters to go to schools and become educated. Afghan society is still a male-dominated society. People do not believe in the power of their daughters. They think that only boys can do anything and have the capability, an issue that is painful for me.

*Thank you to Sahar for connecting me with Halima.*

# Jocelyne

**19** years old

Kinshasa, Democratic Republic of the Congo

**What are your hobbies?**
ASMR [a form of relaxation through watching calming videos] and music, writing, and sports. Music helps me to relax and to think about my life.

**Tell us about your family, your brothers and sisters.**
I live with 6 brothers and sisters from the same parents. I'm the oldest one, Denise is in fashion school, Maria studies literacy, Elyse and Anderson are still in middle school, Consolala is in kindergarten, and the last one is a baby named Xiao Jedu, which means "Little Jesus" in Chinese. He is not born yet.

**What are your favorite subjects?**
My favorites classes are anatomic and the pathologies [diseases] because when you study pathologies, I find it interesting that you always find a specific cure given the symptoms. Specific parts of the body have different symptoms and with these symptoms you can give the right cure. It's really fascinating.

Kinshasa,
Democratic Republic of the Congo

# "Life is hard here but people from the neighborhood helped me."

**IN HER FREE TIME,** Jocelyne likes to listen to music and ask herself important questions about life. Some of her favorites include:

- *Where I'm at now?*
- *Where will I go?*
- *What will I do about my life?*
- *Who I'm hanging with? Are they a good influence? Do I learn from them?*
- *What will I accomplish for me and the society?*
- *What is the stage of my relationship with God?*

Jocelyne also loves writing. "When I write, I can really say what I want to say without anyone judging me or hurting somebody. I just try to write to keep the original meaning of my ideas," she says. "But [my] studies are more important because my dream is to save lives. For me it's like being a hero."

She's a student in her second year of college, getting her undergraduate degree in nursing at Institut Supérieur en Sciences Infirmières, or the Higher Institution of Nursing Sciences. In addition to attending classes and studying, she also has an internship where she cares for patients.

Her days are especially long and stressful when she has to go to her internship: she leaves for work before anyone else at home wakes up and returns at the end of the day just two hours before bedtime.

Jocelyne lives in the capital city of the Democratic Republic of Congo (DRC) with her father, a mechanical engineer; her mother, a maid; and her six younger brothers and sisters. ◊

**"LIFE IS HARD HERE,"** Jocelyne writes, describing going to a well one morning to collect water.

"I would say that life in Kinshasa, and that's what I know, is a daily adventure. Transport, water, and electricity are not always guaranteed, which is an additional difficulty to face every day," agrees Olga Tauler San Miguel, a nurse and academic secretary at the Institut Supérieur en Sciences Infirmières, where Jocelyne studies.

These difficulties are not atypical in the DRC—even though the country is rich in minerals and precious metals, the economic inequality is significant, and it ranks as one of the poorest countries in the world, with a poverty rate of 73 percent.[55]

Many young people here have grown up against a backdrop of ongoing conflict and violence that has claimed millions of lives and displaced millions of people.[56] A civil war that lasted from 1997 to 2003 killed more than five million people.[57]

And tens of thousands of children[58]—about a third of them girls, according to some reports[59]—were recruited or abducted to become child soldiers. While there has been a fragile peace since the 2000s, some renewed violence has taken place in recent years.[60] As of 2018, more than 13 million people in the country needed humanitarian assistance, and more than 4.5 million people from the DRC were displaced, or forced to leave their homes.[61]

But the DRC is a large country—about the size of Western Europe[62]—and Jocelyne lives in Kinshasa, in the western part of the country. Much of the violence and horror unfolded in the east, a long way from her home. ◊

*Translated from French*

*May 4*

Today was an exhausting day. Saturdays when I'm not at school or at work (internship), I stay at home to help mum to clean the whole house.

At 6 a.m. mum woke me up to tell me to get some water from the well because we don't have any more water. When I got there, a lot of people were already waiting to get some water; then we came back home through the mountains with some heavy bags, it was hard. Life is hard here but people from the neighborhood helped me.

Once I got back home, I cleaned the dishes and mopped up the whole house. When I was done, I went to meet some friends. I was there at 1:55 p.m. and the others only came at 3:21 p.m. Together we waited for the bus which came at 4:03 p.m.

We climbed in the bus and we went to sing religious songs from an old musician in Congo called Lutumba Simaro (he just died on March 30th). The church service started at 7:30 p.m. and ended at 8 p.m. Back home, I was really tired. I cleaned myself and then went to sleep.

✳ ✳ ✳

*May 5*

Today it's Sunday, and my brothers and I get dressed each morning to go to church which is not far from home. We woke up at 6 a.m. to clean up the house and to be ready. I took a bath and went to the church at 8 a.m. (I'm a church singer).

At noon, the church service ended and we had a 30-min rest before the rehearsal, we needed it because we are preparing for a concert called "Legends Never Die" in June. During the rehearsal I was expecting to sing alone sometimes (solo) but it never happened.

What makes me nervous is that it's really hard to manage the rehearsal and the internship at the same time.

When I got back home, I rested a bit because I was really tired and it was a long trip, then I ate, I packed my things for the next day (internship), I washed myself and I went to sleep at 10 p.m. I was with my family in the morning and tonight, so the most interesting part is that even if we face some terrible situations, God and my family are always here for me.

✳ ✳ ✳

*May 6*

Today is really a stressful day, do you know why? Because they came to assess me. I knew it, I had a feeling this morning when I woke up. So, when I started my work day I started to read all the medical files and I wrote my plans to take care of my patients during the day.

At 2:40 p.m. when I was emptying urine from a patient, I saw my teacher. She told me to be ready because she was coming to evaluate my work. I took my internship files; I started to show her all the medical service and told her how many patients and pathologies we had.

Then came the practical part (I already did this before but I was really stressed). Apparently, I did well and my teacher gave me some advice and notes about my practice and about how I should collect data on the patients. She was gone at 2:36 p.m. When I was alone, the stress turned into tiredness, but anyway I did everything I had to do.

I went home stressed and tired; I was sad because I didn't plan this evaluation even if I did my best today. When I told this to my mother she started to laugh. At 9 p.m. we prayed together for all the love God is giving us. When I work as an intern, I see my family only 2 hours during the night, because when I go to work everyone is asleep.

Thank you to the Wonder Foundation and the Institut Supérieur en Sciences Infirmières for connecting me with Jocelyne.

# Luciana

## 16
years old

Guatemala City, Guatemala

### What are your favorite subjects?

My favorite subjects are math and art. I love using my creativity to invent new things and solve problems. I've always been a straight-A student, and I like to be.

### Do you have any hobbies?

After school, I spend most of my time at a ballet studio, where I've been dancing for 9 years now. I met another group of awesome friends here, who have been dancing beside me my whole life.

### What do you want to do when you grow up?

Since I was 8, I've been interested in pursuing a career in fashion design. I've taken sewing classes and even made a cocktail dress I'm pretty proud of. However, I am still exploring my options, as new careers are emerging every year.

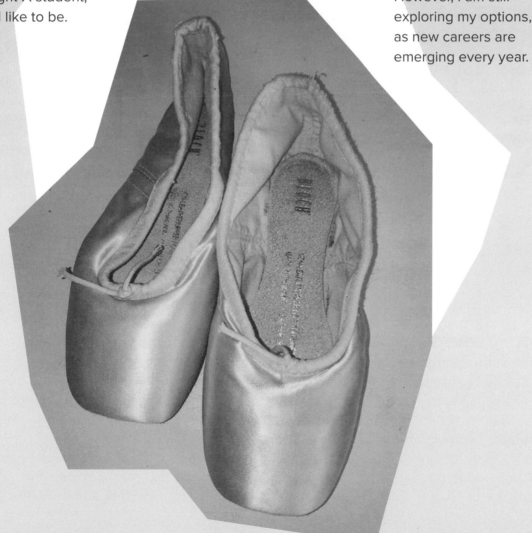

# "I love using my creativity to invent new things and solve problems."

**"MY ULTIMATE GOAL** is to be successful, happy, and give back to my beautiful country," says Luciana.

The sixteen-year-old lives with her parents, César and Maria, and her younger brother, Thomas, all of whom she's close to. She attends a bilingual school—studying in Spanish and English—in Guatemala, loves math and art, and is a straight-A student. Luciana has been dancing ballet since she was five years old, and she spends most of her time outside of school at the studio.

Her creativity extends beyond dance—Luciana has been taking sewing classes, and although she's still exploring career options, one of her hopes is to become a fashion designer.

Guatemala City,
Guatemala

She's sociable and has a lot of friends, and she's also a hardworking student who gets good grades and enjoys academic achievement.

One of her proudest accomplishments is winning the Destination Imagination tournament—she's part of a seven-person team that has been participating in this international competition every year since 2014. More than 150,000 people compete in the tournament, which includes academic challenges in several different categories, and Luciana's team won first place in the Guatemalan national tournament this year.[63] A few years ago, her team won the global finals of this competition, which Luciana describes as "one of the best experiences of our lives."

"The Guatemalan selection was tiny compared to other countries and states," she remembers. "But when our flag appeared on the big screen, announcing that our team had won, the entire world paid attention . . . We were jumping and screaming and hugging and crying. The name 'Guate!' being chanted in unison is all that I remember before running towards the stage to receive our medals and trophy. I couldn't believe we had defeated the entire world, and I still can't." ◊

**THE LIFE LUCIANA DESCRIBES—** surprise parties, preparing for her confirmation (a Catholic religious rite), doctor's appointments—paints a very different picture of life in Guatemala than what you might read if you've been following international news in the last few years. Guatemala regularly makes the news because of gang violence (the country has one of the world's highest rates of homicide[64] and femicide—or the killing of women because of their gender[65]), unemployment, poverty (about 60 percent of Guatemalans live below the poverty line[66]), and how climate change is leading to economic and food insecurity.[67]

Additionally, headlines from Guatemala and neighboring El Salvador and Nicaragua in recent years have often focused on migration: Record numbers of people, including children traveling on their own without parents or older relatives, have been leaving Central America, fleeing violence and poverty. Many of them head to the United States for asylum.[68] In 2019, headlines in the United States and across the world were flooded with photos and stories of these migrants and the horrific and inhumane camps and conditions they faced at the border and upon crossing into the United States.

The adversities that many Guatemalans have fled are not reflected

in the Guatemala you will see throug Luciana's eyes—not that any of the girl in this book are meant to represent a the voices, experiences, or stories o girls in their country or community. I a country with one of the highest rate of economic inequality in the regior poverty and violence coexist with mor comfortable lives like Luciana's.[69] ◊

*Monday, April 8, 2019*

My day started as normal as usual. I woke up at 5:45, caught the bus at 6:30, and had a normal school day. When I got home, my plan was to go to my ballet class. However, my mom had scheduled an appointment with the ophthalmologist to make sure that everything was okay with my brother's eyesight and my own. My mom had been wanting to take me for a while now, since I frequently have headaches. I figured it was from all the stress, due to the intensity of my past few weeks. Anyway, she took us to get examined. When we got to the clinic, I was confident about my eyesight, and that my mom was overreacting. I was wrong.

During my eye exam, I was shocked that I wasn't able to recognize a small row of letters. I thought an F was a P, and a C was an O. The number row was even worse, as I couldn't identify any of them confidently. Instead of being upset, however, I started laughing so much that I needed to dry my eyes to keep going. I was going to wear glasses and was kind of excited to choose them. In the process of trying them on, I kept laughing while thinking about how terrible and "nerdy" I looked. I knew my friends were going to tease me. My mom reassured me that all of that was a lie, but she's my mom. So that's her job. Anyhow, I went for a pair of red glasses. I liked them and decided to never let anyone influence that thought.

*Tuesday, April 9, 2019*

Today I got the best news I could ask for. For the last year, my family has been going through some rough times. My aunt Denisse was diagnosed with cancer in July of 2018. Because of this, she had to spend most of her time away in Florida, where she was getting treatment. She went through chemotherapy, surgery, and radiation therapy, but thanks to all our prayers, she finally finished her treatment today. Denisse will return to Guatemala as a cancer-free woman! While waiting for the bus this morning, my brother and I sent an audio message congratulating her. I'm sure she received many similar ones. I spent the whole day looking at pictures of her last day at the hospital and colorful posts saying, "WE DID IT!"

My confirmation is coming up in a few weeks, and I've asked my aunt to be my godmother. I chose her because I believe she is a strong role model, and I admire her for who she is. I knew she would kick cancer's butt, so I feel really happy to have her by my side during one of the most important days of my life. I have picked my dress and shoes, and am excited for this day to come. I'm worried about speaking, though. My mom signed me up to read a little excerpt in mass. I've done this before but always talk too fast or mess up. I hope I can pull it off. But that's something to worry about tomorrow. Right now, I just feel blessed to enjoy this moment with my family, and I keep praying that we won't have to face this struggle ever again.

*Friday, April 12, 2019*

I LOVE surprise birthday parties!

I guess it's probably because I've enjoyed my own so much. When I turned 15, my family and close friends threw a surprise for me. On my birthday, they woke me up with confetti, Silly String, presents, and a group of mariachis singing "Los Mañanitas." I was so excited, and never expected it! On top of the morning celebration, there was a surprise party I was unaware of. Two days later, my whole family and a large group of friends, everybody singing "Happy Birthday." I had the most amazing time and will always remember it.

I remembered this because I went to my friend's surprise party today and was one of the last people to leave. After having lunch at the restaurant, we headed over to another friend's house. As the hours passed, there were fewer of us left. When we were only 4 and the sun was down, we stayed in the middle of the golf course singing our hearts out. I had the best time, surrounded by my best friends.

*Thank you to Girl Up for connecting me with Luciana.*

# Mandisa

## 18
years old

Durban, South Africa

**What are your favorite subjects in school?**
English, life sciences, dramatic arts, history, and geography

**What do you like doing when you're not at school?**
I love spending time chilling at home, watching a comedy movie with my family, and sharing some jokes.

**Tell us about your friends.**
My friends' names are Thobeka and Minenhle. We are in the same grade and in the same class. When we are together we share jokes and they share their experiences in life, about how they have made mistakes and learned from them. We also do our homework together after school because we enjoy each other's company.

# "I want to be an independent woman. I want to be my own woman and be self-made."

**"MY NUMBER ONE DREAM** is to be a lawyer: I want to be an independent woman, I want to be my own woman and be self-made," says Mandisa.

She lives in KwaMashu township in Durban, South Africa, with her mother, sister, two nieces, and two nephews. She's been raised by her mother, who is a single parent and mother of four children, two of whom have passed away. In addition to law, Mandisa is also considering becoming a social worker or a nurse, but this all depends on how well she does on her matric, or matriculation, which is the equivalent in South Africa of a high school diploma.

Mandisa hopes that when she grows up, she can "fulfill my mother's dream of living in a big house where she can have her own room, sleep on her own bed, have everything in her room that she needs, and have a fully furnished kitchen where she can cook and enjoy her kitchen."

After fulfilling her mother's dream, "it will be my turn," Mandisa says, "to fufill my dreams of having a house, car, but not just any house, the kind of house I want and the kind of car I want." ◊

**WHILE MANDISA SHARES** her hopes and dreams, she also writes about a classmate whose plans were thwarted when she got pregnant. Her friend had to drop out of school, and she faced a lot of shame and judgment from her community.

This type of shame, which young mothers across the world are often subjected to, can affect whether they stay in school, what types of jobs and other future opportunities might be available to them, and how much support they can seek from their communities.

And while the shame young mothers face is specific, girls and women across cultures and continents are taught shame from an early age: shame about their bodies, their ambition, their sexuality, and the space they occupy in the world. In English, we even have a vocabulary of shame: *slut shaming, body shaming, walk of shame*, and more.

In some parts of Africa—the continent with the highest teenage pregnancy rates in the world, according to the United Nations[70]—the shame and stigma of being a teen mother has been written into the law, limiting the opportunities and support available to them. For example, until 2020, in Tanzania, Equatorial Guinea, and Sierra Leone, pregnant girls or young mothers are banned from going to government-run schools.[71]

Durban,
South Africa

Pregnancy can literally be the end of a girl's education, as was almost the case with Mandisa's friend. But South Africa is one of twenty-six African countries that has laws in place to help young mothers return to school after giving birth, and the government provides social and financial support for teenage moms.[72] Despite the law, the judgment and disdain from adults and organizations in the community can keep teen moms out of school.

"They won't be forced to drop out of school, there is a legislation, but it's just their own stigma and also maybe parents feel ashamed for their child going to school and pregnant, so they will then encourage them not to go to school or the girl herself will feel like she does not fit in any longer because there's stigma and other children will mock her," explains Mpendulo Nyembe, the executive director of uMthombo, an organization in Durban that works with youth. ◊

*Tuesday*

Dear Diary,

I woke up at 6:15 a.m. I was running late but prepared to go to school and was ready at 7:15. I didn't have breakfast, because if I had, I would have been late, but I walked fast to school and I wasn't late. Today I was looking forward to the presentation in history. Ten students were supposed to read [about] a new topic and analyze and tell the class what they learnt.

When I went to class today, I met up with my friends and had a morning talk before the class started, where we discussed our homework and saw how we wrote it. If you wrote something wrong, we corrected each other by showing you the steps and making you understand.

The day went on great and drama was the last period. We practiced until 3:00 p.m. and it was worth it. It was very fun, group members practicing the scene work.

Then I came back home, did my chores, and wrote my homework. After that, I watched a TV series and went to bed at 9:00 p.m.

✳ ✳ ✳

*Wednesday*

Dear Diary,

I woke up at 6:00 a.m. and prepared to go to school, made my bed and I was ready at 7:00 a.m., had breakfast and finished at 7:15 and went to school. Reached school at 7:35 and an assembly was full of pupils and teachers talking to them on what was going to happen for the day.

Today I was looking forward to drama practice as we were going to learn new moves on movement and some of the group members changed their individual piece and some changed their scene work. I was looking forward to saying my individual piece today. When I did my individual piece, our instructor said I did it well and I should keep it up and practice more.

I spent time with my friends after the second period when the teachers went to a meeting. We sat and talked about how life is and the challenges they have faced. While we were talking some of our classmates engaged in our conversation, and one of them told us about her mistake when she fell pregnant and they chased her out of her home and the father of the child said that the baby wasn't his. She had nowhere to go when her aunt told her to come to her house and stay with her, but she had to drop out of school because she was pregnant and had to give birth before she went back to school. Life was tough for her at that time because she was doing grade 11 and passed for grade 12 and it got delayed. Luckily for her after she gave birth to her baby, her aunt sent her to school to continue her studies and finish matric [secondary school qualifications] and they accepted her at school. Now the lesson I learnt was don't do something you will regret later and might cost you big time.

My day today was very good, got to hear people sharing their stories and how difficult life is and I learnt something from them. When I got home today everything was done and we all sat down and watched TV series and drank some hot tea and watched a movie because it was cold and it was raining. I went to bed very early, it was 8:00 p.m.

✳ ✳ ✳

*Thursday*

Dear Diary,

Today I woke up at 6:00 a.m. as usual and prepared to go to school. I was ready at 7:00 and had no breakfast today. I drank tea and went to school; at least I drank some tea. Reached school at 7:30 and went to the assembly, our principal announced that home time will be early today because our teachers were preparing for the Easter holidays and some of them were going to church.

You know, I was looking forward to the life science class today because we were supposed to finish the topic and start a new one. So, school ended at 11:30 a.m. today, but I didn't go home, I only went home at 1:30 p.m. because we had to stay back for our rehearsals and they went on very well. No one was arguing with anyone, everything went smoothly.

When I came back home, I put on my high heels and practiced some modeling as I enjoy doing it every once in a while because I love modeling so much. I just enjoy it, but I had to put it on hold because I am doing matric and it would have added some stress and I try to avoid stress every chance I get, because I'm always laughing and making people around me laugh, so if I'm stressed, who's going to make them laugh?

I can just say today was just a day, a normal day, nothing exciting about it, now as they say, every day is different. I went to bed at 10:00 p.m. because I don't have to go to school tomorrow because Easter holidays are starting.

*Thank you to uMthombo for connecting me with Mandisa.*

# Marta

## 14
### years old

Milan, Italy

### Tell us about your family.

My mum's name is Guendalina and she's a social worker. My dad's name is Fabrizio and he works in a hotel: he is a chef. I have a sister, Constanza, she is 6 years old, and she's in the first year of elementary school. I have a brother, Matteo, he is 11 years old. He's in the last year of elementary school.

### What do you want to do when you grow up?

I would like to become a surgeon when I grow up, but I'm not sure.

### What are your hobbies?

When I'm not studying, I go out with my friends or I play with my brother and sister or I watch TV.

"Today I returned to Milan. I'm a bit sad because I wanted to stay in Rome some more. I had a lot of fun: every day my aunt Betty and I had a walk in the neighborhood . . . we sat at the table talking about everything that came to mind."

Milan,
Italy

**MARTA STARTED** high school this year. It's been an adjustment so far: "I get on well with both my classmates and my professors, but I still have to get used to, and learn to, get better organized for studying," she explains.

Marta lives in Milan with her parents and her younger brother and sister. She is also close to her extended family and writes about the time she spends with her cousins and aunt and uncles. She writes in her diary about spending time with her family in Rome, a welcome break from a stressful school year.

Most of Marta's days are spent at school—she goes to a science high school and her favorite subject is math. One of the biggest adjustments in this new school has been making friends.

"As of now I haven't established great friendships," she says. She has known most of her closest friends her entire life—she met her best friends Carola in the first grade and Margherita in nursery school.

She's also close to her cousin Bianca. "She's 15 years old," Marta says, "I've known her since I was born. We often fight but nevertheless, I love her very much."

But in a new school without her old friends, she has to find new ones. ◊

**MARTA LIVES IN MILAN,** the second largest city in Italy, after Rome. It's the country's financial and cultural hub and is known for its vibrant fashion industry. In addition to hosting one of the big global fashion weeks every year, Milan is home to about 90 museums, more than 190 art galleries, and nearly 60 theaters and concert halls. Nearly 189,000 creative workers are based in Milan, as are about half of Italy's publishing houses.[73]

The city's economy is also centered on tech, design, and innovation. A significant amount of foreign investment drives growth and development in Milan, and the city is set to host the Winter Olympics in 2026.[74]

*Monday, March 4, 2019*

Today was an easy day. I woke up at 6:30 a.m. because I wanted to revise [study] for the epic oral test [epic is a subject involving the study of epic poems like the *Iliad* or *Odyssey*]. I got up from my bed at 7:50 a.m. and I managed to take the bus by the skin of my teeth! I started school at 8:15 a.m. In the first hour I had epic, and luckily I wasn't quizzed! But she said she will do the oral test tomorrow . . .

Then I had Latin, but I revised for the science oral test because today is 4th and she always gives the oral test to the person whose surname corresponds to the day and . . . I'm the 4th! Later I did English and after, in the last hour, I did science and she didn't quiz me. Today the science teacher, strangely, didn't use her method to decide who would do the oral test, but picked 3 random people.

After that I had lunch at the school bar with my classmates, because we organized to remain at school to revise math, in order to prepare ourselves for the test. We started studying at 2:30 p.m. and continued until 6:00 p.m. Then I went home. I was feeling a little bad so I measured my temperature and I had 37.2°C [99°F]. I tried to continue to study both for math and epic but I was not able to; I was feeling too sick so I went to bed. Tomorrow I have the math test and I hope to do it well.

*Saturday, March 9, 2019*

Today I returned to Milan. I'm a bit sad because I wanted to stay in Rome some more. I had a lot of fun: every day my aunt Betty and I had a walk in the neighborhood, and then we returned home and after that, she helped me with my homework. In the remaining hours we sat at the table talking about everything that came to mind. I really needed those days with her . . . because this first year of high school is destroying me.

Yesterday night, I, my aunt Betty, my cousin, and my uncles went out for dinner in a Chinese restaurant; it was very funny, I liked spending that night with them so much.

Today I left Rome at 2:00. My aunt Betty and my uncle Carlo accompanied me to the station, and I arrived in Milan at 5:00, where my dad and my sister picked me up. After that I spent the evening playing with my sister and watching TV. They were unforgettable days. I had a lot of fun and I hope I didn't annoy my uncles too much. I can't wait until school finishes in order to be able to see my uncles and my cousin again. Only 89 days left!

# Merisena

## 13
### years old

Cité Soleil, Haiti

**What do you like doing for fun?**
Sometimes, if there is electricity, we take a little time to watch TV with the family.

**What do you like to do after school?**
I always finish studying at 4 p.m. After, there are days that I train in chess, days I train in volleyball, and days I train in soccer. I'm doing pretty well in all these disciplines.

**Tell us about your family.**
I live in a family of 11 members, my mother and my father and 9 children, 4 boys and 5 girls. I am the fourth child. My mother sells candles. My father sells brooms, and he has to walk around several kilometers every day with the brooms so he can get home with a little money.

## "I don't live in a rich family, but I love my family so much because my mother and my father make a lot of effort for us."

**IN A HOUSE OFTEN** caught in the midst of gunfire and gang violence, in one of the poorest neighborhoods in the poorest country in the Western Hemisphere,[75] lives a thirteen-year-old chess champion.

Meet Merisena.

She lives in Cité Soleil (which means Sun City in English), a neighborhood in Port au Prince, Haiti, with her four brothers, four sisters, and parents. She's grown up in a country that's made headlines around the world in her lifetime for a series of horrors—more than 60 percent of Haiti's population lives in poverty,[76] and in 2010 the country was devastated by a catastrophic earthquake. The disaster left more than 200,000 people dead and 1.5 million people without homes.[77] It was followed by a cholera epidemic that killed about 10,000 people.[78]

Merisena's diary entries give us a small peak into what daily life, and daily challenges, look like in Cité Soleil. She writes about her family not being able to afford more than one meal a day, power cuts (this year, long blackouts have become common, and as of May 2019, a few months after Merisena wrote her diary entries, much of Haiti was getting only about three hours of electricity a day[79]), and the "civil war"—what she calls the ongoing gang violence in her neighborhood. The month she was writing the diary entries she shared with us, gunfire regularly echoed through the streets around her home.

But Merisena's life isn't just her circumstances, isn't just the poverty and violence she's growing up in. She trains in chess most days after school and competes in tournaments. She has big dreams for the future—she studies hard to make her parents proud, and so that she can do more when she grows up.

"I never stop thinking about my dream of becoming a nurse to help my family and take care of people in the community," she says. ◊

Cité Soleil,
Haiti

**BECAUSE OF ONGOING** violence in Cité Soleil, Merisena can't always leave home during the day for safety reasons.

"She would listen to all the gunshots and sometimes it would be really hard for her to go to school because to cross the street, you could be in the middle of gunfire without knowing," explains Daniel Tillias, co-founder of Sakala, which is a youth community center and organization that supports the development of children, including Merisena, in Cité Soleil.

Growing up in a neighborhood known for gang violence doesn't just affect safety, it also affects how the rest of the world views you.

"The neighborhood is quite stigmatized," says Tillias. "And people are scared that if you are a girl from Cité Soleil it means that you are something wrong—you must be involved in stealing, you must be involved in any kind of bad behavior that creates this mistrust towards you."

Merisena struggles with this, too. Even though she's a chess champion who competes across the country, she finds that people still make assumptions about her. "I don't like the neighborhood where I live, because when you tell someone that you live in Cité Soleil, he discriminates against you, he doesn't look at you like a person," she explains.

This is very common, according to Tillias. "That's one thing that slows [girls from the neighborhood] in their progress, because they're not well accepted outside of the community, they're not well-received . . . you're from Cité Soleil, that's very common, people expect you're either the girlfriend of a gangster or you're a gangster yourself," he says. ◊

*Translated from Creole*

Every day I get up at 5 a.m. to get ready to go to school and help with some work at home. I leave school at noon, I take a little break after to help my mother with some work, and after that I go to study in Sakala, an organization in the area that supports children and young people. I always finish studying at 4 p.m., and after that I have to train in chess or soccer.

I go back home at 6 p.m. At this time if there is electricity I watch TV, we share jokes between us, or we play. My family doesn't have much money: sometimes we eat once a day, rarely we eat twice a day.

My mother sells candles. She can spend several days before making a profit of $1 and 10 cents. My father sells brooms. He has to walk several kilometers every day with the brooms so that he can get home with a little money.

My father goes out at 7 a.m. to sell in the four corners of the country. It's only when my father returns in the afternoon that my mother will cook for us to eat.

I don't live in a rich family, but I love my family so much because my mother and my father make a lot of effort for us and often they make us sit down to explain to us how we should behave in society.

Sometimes I don't feel good because of the insecurity that there is in the country. There are days when my father goes out, I pray to God to protect him because I know the situation of the country.

The area where we live is Cité Soleil. Often there is shooting: sometimes children can't go to school, hospitals can't work, people are forced to stay at home because of the civil war.

I feel very bad when I live these bad moments; sometimes I cry.

In the neighborhood, many children can't go to school because their parents don't have money. My mom and my dad made a lot of sacrifices for me to send me to school. Even though my school is not expensive, sometimes it happens that I am sent back from school for nonpayment of school fees.

I strive to work well at school to get good grades, because of all the efforts my parents make for me.

I have some friends with whom I usually speak. Sometimes we share our dreams, but sometimes we have problems talking because the civil war in the area prevents us from meeting.

I don't like the neighborhood where I live, because when you tell someone that you live in Cité Soleil, he discriminates against you, he doesn't look at you like a person.

Despite the difficult situations, I fight to become a nurse so that my mother and father will be proud of me, and to help them too.

✳   ✳   ✳

I often take a little time to think when I'm at home, especially when there is shooting in the area when the gangs clash with each other, which means people can't go to their activities, schools, hospitals, can't work. My father goes out every day to fetch food for the house; and there's no need to tell you that when there is disorder in the streets, it's very hard for the family to eat. I think about it when I'm at school, also when I'm in Sakala, but I think about it more when I'm at home.

Whenever I think about these things, I have problems. I wonder why I couldn't live in another country, why my family could not have money, especially when we are hungry and when there is civil war in the area. So I think I need to work more at school so that I can become a nurse so that I can help my family and the community. I often ask God to let me leave the area because there is too much violence and I watch many other girls in the neighborhood fall into bad acts.

Although I am growing up in an area where there is a lot of violence, although I am in a family where there is no money, an area where most girls get pregnant or fall into bad acts, and when you tell someone that you live in this area, you are subject to all bad things, they humiliate you. Despite all these things, I never stop thinking that one day I can raise my family and my community too.

*Thank you to Sakala for connecting me with Merisena.*

# Miriam

## 16
### years old

Sundsvall, Sweden

### What instruments do you play?

My main instruments are percussion as well as guitar. That includes not only regular drum set playing, but classical percussion such as marimba, tambourine, and snare drum, too.

### Do you play any other instruments?

I can also play a bit of piano, bass guitar, ukulele, melodica, and violin, but I don't consider myself a pianist, etc.

### What kinds of music do you play?

At school we usually play classical pieces for percussion ensemble, symphony orchestra, or just solo pieces. In the band I'm in back in Sundsvall, we play My Chemical Romance–type music, but what I've written on my own is mostly solo pieces for guitar or vibraphone.

## "I don't like to be known for just one part of me . . . It feels like it hollows out everything else that I do, like that one thing is all that I do."

**"I DON'T LIKE** to be known for just one part of me," says Miriam. "For example, my liking people regardless of gender or playing instruments. It feels like it hollows out everything else that I do, like that one thing is all that I do."

Miriam lives in a city in northern Sweden with her parents, Annika and Kenneth, her sister, Alva, and their dog, Tyson. She shared diary entries from 2018 for the "Girlhood Around the World" series that originally ran in *The Lily*. I've

Sundsvall,
Sweden

included some of those entries, as well as entries she shared from 2019. In 2018, she was applying to certified music schools for the final years of high school, after attending the school in her hometown of Sundsvall for nine years. In 2019, she wrote from her new school in Falun, to which she had applied and where she was accepted into the music conservatory.

These certified music schools are highly specialized, and admission is very competitive. "This sets a very high standard on the musical level of the students, whereas regular programs are open to anyone, even people who haven't played an instrument before," Miriam says. "There is also a lot of free time during the school day to make time for practice, and the special programs also have some courses that regular music programs don't." ◊

**MIRIAM IS GROWING UP** in a country that claims to have the world's first "feminist government" and ranks third on the United Nations' Gender Inequality Index, making it one of the most advanced countries in the world for women's empowerment and economic status.[80] When it comes to LGBTQ rights, Sweden is ranked fourth out of 49 countries in Europe by ILGA-Europe.[81] But even though Sweden is one of the most accepting countries of LGBTQ rights, a 2019 report on LGBTQ youth in Sweden found that LGBTQ people report poorer health, have increased risk of mental health problems, and still can face hate crimes.[82]

One way in which LGBTQ youth around the world deal with feeling unsafe in public spaces is by turning to virtual spaces and finding community online. More than 60 percent of LGBTQ youth have used the Internet to connect with other LGBTQ people.[83] It's a way to find people with shared identities and experiences, and to get information, explains a.t. furuya, the Gay, Lesbian & Straight Education Network's (GLSEN) Youth Programs Manager.

This is certainly true for Miriam. Some of the friends she mentions— Anja, Annika, and Jenny—are people she has met online: through comments on mutual friends' Instagram posts, through shared interests online, and in Instagram communities for LGBTQ girls and women.

"I have met a lot of friends via Instagram, which can be easier at times because you can find people with similar views or interests," Miriam explains.

Apps like Instagram and YouTube offer both a chance to meet similar people and to get answers without having to an ask an adult.

"'What does it mean, to come out?' They can figure that out in the privacy of phones, just navigating an app, like Instagram or Tumblr or Twitter," furuya says. "They can watch people transitioning, they can watch people coming out on YouTube, and they can figure out and process without judgment of anyone else."

Growing up, we're often limited to the people we know in our towns or cities, or through our friends and families. But sometimes, a hashtag community or a YouTube channel can show us lives and stories different from those in our immediate communities. ◊

*Miriam participated in the series for* The Lily *and shared diary entries from autumn 2018. I have included excerpts of her diary entries from both autumn 2018 and spring 2019.*

*September 18, 2018*

*9:30 p.m.*

I don't think today was that bad overall. I'm almost over the cold I caught last week, I got a few minutes of extra sleep this morning, and most importantly, I had no serious dips mentally. It was just a good Tuesday. My usual Tuesday activities went well too. I learned some things during my percussion lesson and I learned how much better I've gotten at reading sheet music during orchestra practice.

The most important thing that happened to me today was that I got a letter from the hospital in Umea, regarding a few appointments. I need to be diagnosed with a specific condition in order to get help with my mental health, and so as this is the first step to getting help with that, I'm really excited. I've waited so many months for this letter, and much, much longer before that because I was afraid to tell my parents how I felt and that I needed medical help. I cried when I saw the envelope and where it was from.

I'm sort of stressed about an event coming up in less than two weeks. I have a gig booked Friday the 28th, and I'm going to play my own music that I've written for vibraphone and guitar. Only problem is, I feel like I need one or two more songs for vibraphone, and I'm not sure if I'll be able to finish the one I have started in time, as I'll be busy this weekend. I'm sure it'll be fine though. Maybe I'm a bit stressed over school too.

*September 23, 2018*

*10:31 p.m.*

As I'm writing this, I'm on the train back from Stockholm, where I've been since Thursday afternoon. I'm tired and thirsty, but I still have around an hour and a half until I'm back home. I did choose the latest possible train I could take though; I wanted to have as much time as possible with my friend Ivan who lives in Stockholm, and I definitely think that's worth losing a little bit of sleep for just one night.

This weekend has been so tiring, but so, so fun. On Friday, I visited a school. It definitely gave me an idea of what the school's like, but it also showed me what actually can be different from school to school. I've been attending the same school since I was six years old; I had absolutely no clue what another school could be like. Before the visit, my whole vision of the school was based on what my percussion teacher had told me and what the school's website said. I was almost completely sure I wanted to go there, but now after my visit, I'm much more uncertain about everything, and I think I need to visit a few more schools before making my decision.

I've developed a huge crush on a special somebody, and it's actually driving me mad. She's just . . . so kind. I literally can't stop thinking about her; she's on my mind every waking minute and it's making it very difficult to focus on anything else. I spent a whole hour during school on Thursday thinking about her and when I arrived at Ivan's house on Friday afternoon after the visit to the school, I cried because she's such an angel and it makes me sad that she'll probably never like me back because I'm a girl! I wish I could hold her hand forever but oh well, maybe some day.

✳ ✳ ✳

*March 28, 2019*
*8:11 p.m.*

I'm currently on the train home from Falun, a city 4 hours by train away from home. There's a school that I'd love to attend over there which I auditioned for today. I've applied for the composition program and the classical percussion program; I really hope I get in!

Two of my online friends live close to Falun. I'd hoped to see at least one of them during the time between the end of the tests and when my train home departed, but both of them were busy, unfortunately. I've only met them once each before, Annika when I visited Falun last time. I went in December just to see that the school was as good as it sounded. I didn't want to apply for a school just to see when I get there that it isn't any good just like the one in

Stockholm. I met my other friend, Anja, after a concert in Stockholm. We were coincidentally both going to see Twenty One Pilots in February, so we decided to meet up after the concert. We could only talk during the short metro ride, but if I move to Falun this autumn I'll be able to see her tons more!

✳ ✳ ✳

April 14, 2019<br>10:42 p.m.

I have had such. A. Great. Weekend.

Yesterday, there was this thing called UKM, or Ung Kultur Möts (Young Culture Meets) in Sundsvall. It's this festival where anyone can sign up to do anything they want on stage, or to show off anything you've made in an exhibition. There's a jury who then picks a couple of those who perform or show what they've made, who get to go to the regional festival, and after that, there's a slight chance you can go to the national festival, which is in late June. I performed with my solo project Miriam Rain, where I play instrumental music for guitar and vibraphone (not at the same time though—yet). The jury enjoyed what I did, so I'm going to be one of lucky performers in Örnsköldsvik, where the regional festival is!

Before the sound check and all the preparations for UKM, I had band rehearsal with my friend Vera for her solo project where I'm her accompanying drummer. My crush (not the same one that I wrote about a few months ago) happens to play piano in the band as well, so the rehearsals are usually what I look forward to most every week. We usually leave and all go our separate ways after rehearsals, but since both me and her were going to do things shortly after in the music school, we both brought food and had lunch together! Aaahh!! It's impossible to not be filled to the brim with happiness when I'm around her to be honest. She's so SWEET and amazing and just, I can't even describe her.

That's not all that was great about this weekend though. My friend Jenny who lives in Umeå came down to visit me. She arrived by train 30 minutes before yesterday's event started, and I went to the station to meet up with her. I made sure to not have to perform first, so it wouldn't be such a hurry to get back to the venue. It was her first time seeing me perform live, and as a result I really tried to make sure she and everyone else new in the audience would get a great first experience of my music. After the event, we went home to my place and watched a movie before going to sleep.

# Naya

16 years old

Berlin, Germany, and Damascus, Syria

**What are your favorite subjects?**
I am really interested in the natural sciences, specifically biology and physics.

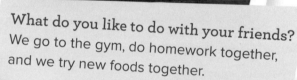

**What do you like to do with your friends?**
We go to the gym, do homework together, and we try new foods together.

**Do you have any hobbies?**
Other than traveling, I love being artistic and creative through painting and dancing. I have gone to street dance classes for 3 years.

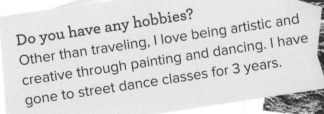

"I did not want to leave my home country, my friends, my room, and most of my possessions . . . I always had the dream that I would graduate in Syria and go through all of my school years with my friends."

**WHEN NAYA WAS** thirteen years old, her parents decided to leave their home in Damascus, Syria, and head to Germany.

"I did not want to leave my home country, my friends, my room, and most of my possessions," Naya remembers. "I did not see the problem as my parents saw it. I always had the dream that I would graduate in Syria and go through all of my school years with my friends."

Her family left Syria because of the ongoing war. Since 2011, hundreds of

Damascus,
Syria

Berlin,
Germany

a new language. And, she adds, she didn't even like the German soccer team!

"The first year was a bit stressful and rough, as I could not speak English well enough to socialize confidently. So, I avoided many social interactions and focused on my studies," Naya said. "Unlike most people who immigrated to Germany, I did not repeat any grades, which was beneficial, but also challenging."

Her parents had to deal with change, too. They worked in accounting and business management in Syria, but they are now taking various courses, and her dad is a part-time tax advisor.

But now, Naya says, Berlin feels like home. ◊

thousands of people have been killed or injured, and millions—like Naya's family—have had to flee for their safety, as their homes and hometowns were turned into battlefields.

For Naya, moving away from home meant not only feeling sad about leaving behind friends, family, and a familiar life, it also meant adjusting to life in a new country—and the many changes and challenges that came along with it.

Naya, who grew up speaking and learning Arabic, remembers that, at first, she didn't want to move to Germany because she was worried about learning

**WHEN PEOPLE FLEE** their homes because of war, violence, or persecution, they are called refugees. According to official data, there are more than six million Syrian refugees in the world.

The story of refugees is a defining narrative of our time—there are 26 million refugees worldwide.[84] Many of them—13 million—are children.[85] The reasons refugees leave their home countries could include war or violence that make life dangerous, or because they have a well-founded fear they could experience violence because of their race, ethnicity, sexuality, or political or religious beliefs.

News stories in recent years have featured the struggles refugees sometimes face while fleeing for safety: long lines of families walking hundreds of miles through the desert, people on overcrowded rafts sailing across the Mediterranean Sea to safety in Europe, and communities living in refugee camps with no certainty for the future and no country or city to call home.

Every migrant and refugee family's journey is different, and not all involve the most trying physical journeys we see in the headlines. But all refugees, displaced people, and asylum seekers have one thing in common: they had to leave home because home was no longer safe. ◊

*April 8, 2019*

Dear Diary,

Today, I woke up at 7 a.m., kind of late but I still had half an hour to eat something and get ready for another week of school. Sadly, I did not have time to enjoy a cup of tea. It was not an ideal morning, because when I have to hurry up in the morning, I can't take the time to wake up properly and then I get sleepy during the day. So for that reason, I was not excited to go to school, especially since it is Monday, like honestly who does not hate Mondays.

But it is a start of the last week before break, I couldn't wait until the day was over. Four more days till break; I hope it passes by quickly. I started off the day by evaluating some economic policies that deal with unemployment in economics class. It was not a bad lesson, it was more a chill lesson as we were discussing and expressing our opinions on the issue. Then followed three hours of English, it is the most boring lesson on earth; 3 hours of listening and concentrating on *The Great Gatsby*. I am happy that I only have English once a week. I started to get sleepier as the English teacher continued talking and talking. I just could not concentrate anymore. Half the day was over by then, but I still had 2 hours of biology. It is actually the best subject; I really enjoy it and always look forward to it. We discussed the causes and consequences of global warming, which is a crucial problem that we need to consider. Then I got the chance to see my friends and have lunch together. It feels good to share with friends how the day went.

I was really happy that I got the chance to enjoy some sunlight today, so that is a reason to enjoy the rest of the week, if it would stay nice and warm.

After finishing biology at 1:30 p.m., I went home. I had no energy nor motivation to do anything. I just wanted to eat and sleep but at the same time, I have lots of work to do.

✳ ✳ ✳

*April 9, 2019*

Dear diary,

Today I woke up at 7 a.m., as late as yesterday. I woke up feeling jealous of the people who start school later because they can sleep in longer. I was not excited for the day, as it is the longest day of the week: from 8 a.m. till 6:30 p.m. with no free periods in between. It is also the most scientific day of the week, which was this time a headache more than a relief. The weekend was so frustrating that by today I have no energy, no motivation, and can't be efficient anymore.

I started off the day at 8 a.m. by doing a German quiz that I prepared for last minute, but I think it went well; we will see how it goes. Then I had 2 hours of maths, which was boring, but surprisingly we finished a whole chapter in these 2 hours. Then followed 3 hours of physics and 2 hours of biology.

But before I could go home, I had street dance. I love going to street dance as I love socializing with the street dance group and it is a fun and hyperactive class. So I finished at 6:30 p.m. and started to pack my stuff to head home. After street dance, I felt so energetic. Yet, I did not have the motivation to work on the IOC [Individual Oral Commentary, an important exam for high school students], because I find it really hard. I stayed at school with some people who are in my physics class and we discussed random quantum mechanic theories that do not make any sense to us at the moment. We also complained about school and discussed some random topics for about an hour or so. Then I really had to get home, even though I wanted to continue the discussion, because it helped me get out all of the negative energy I had and I was glad that I am not the only person struggling with finishing the IOC. So I went home, showered and had dinner with my family and then at 8:30 I started working on finishing my IOC. By then it was post 10 p.m. and I felt so tired and I directly went to get ready to sleep.

*Thank you to Girls Gearing Up for connecting me with Naya.*

# Raksa

19
years old

Phnom Penh, Cambodia

**Tell us about your friends.**

Most of the time when I am with friends, we like talking about how our lives will come to be in the next five years. Sometimes, my friends and I love cooking food together. I feel bored without them. We have known each other since we were in secondary school and right now we are college students, so we became best friends. They are Phanit, Sreyleak, Chenad, Daneth, and Seyma.

**Tell us about your family.**

My father is a tuk-tuk driver and my mother is a domestic helper. I am very close with my mother. I share all my good and bad news with her; she knows everything about me. I only share good news with my father. However, I love them in equal measure. My parents moved to Phnom Penh when I was 2 to earn a living.

**Who did you live with when your parents left?**

I was left to live with my grandparents in the province. Living with my grandparents is a very joyful memory for life. They treated me like a princess; they sent me to school in the village, and took the best care of me. Besides their farming work, they spent time teaching me basic literacy in addition to my education at school.

# "Living with my grandparents is a very joyful memory ... They treated me like a princess; they sent me to school in the village, and took the best care of me."

Phnom Penh,
Cambodia

**RAKSA IS A** university student in Cambodia's capital city of Phnom Penh. She grew up in the countryside, living in a village in the Prey Veng province with her grandparents.

When she was just two years old, Raksa's parents left their village for Phnom Penh to earn a living—her father as a tuk-tuk driver and her mother as a domestic helper. Since then, her parents and younger brother have lived in the city, and until recently Raksa only saw them when they visited their hometown. "Being separated from your parents for a very young kid is very miserable experience," she says. "I remember the feeling that I was waiting for their visit twice a year during Khmer New Year and Pchum Ben [a Cambodian religious festival], and how hard I cried as a kid every time they went back to the city."

Now, Raksa has made her own version of her parents' journey. She also came to the city for a better life, but instead of working a job, she won a scholarship to a university.

She lives in a dormitory in Phnom Penh run by the Harpswell Foundation, which provides housing for a few promising young women like her from rural areas in Cambodia. And while she has found sisterhood and community with the other girls in the dormitories, Raksa still misses home and her family.

Raksa is the first in her family to attend university. Her parents, as well as the grandparents who raised her, remain committed to her education, and she's studying hard.

This education is just the start. Raksa has a lot more she wants to do.

"I have a dream to become an empowered woman to guide people who have less education, especially women who live in rural or remote areas that suffer from the society and their families," she says. Some of the types of challenges that women living in rural poverty face include widespread gender inequality, lack of access to education, undernutrition, and vulnerability to natural disasters like floods and droughts.[86] ◊

**MORE THAN 70 PERCENT** of Cambodia's population,[87] and about 90 percent of the country's poor,[88] live in rural areas, where access to schools and education can be a challenge, especially for girls.

"In some areas there is not access to schools, high schools in particular. If the school is far away from the home, the parents are afraid to let the child ride a bicycle to school, especially girls," according to Pisey Khim, managing director at the Women's Resource Center in Cambodia, an organization that works to empower women and girls.

Raksa's middle school and high school were about two and half miles from her home. But her family has always been committed to her pursuing an education despite struggles and hardship, so she cycled the distance to and from school every day.

Distance is not the only obstacle preventing girls from finishing school. Sometimes, girls need to get jobs and earn money to help support their families.

"Most of my female friends dropped out after they finished primary or middle school because their family wanted them to help with their farming in the province or to work as garment workers in Phnom Penh for financial support," Raksa says.

This is not uncommon, according to Khim. "Many families cannot afford to send their children to school. Sometimes parents don't understand that education is important for the children, for girls in particular. If a family is expecting their female child to become a housewife, they may believe that there is no need for her to have an education," she explains. ◊

Raksa writes about Songkran, a holiday in Cambodia, in her diary entries.
Here is a little more about the holiday and how it's celebrated.

### What is Songkran / Sankranta?

It's a celebration to mark the start of the Khmer New Year.

### How did you celebrate at your dormitory?

Almost all of us, around 30 students, gathered in the morning, helped each other with the cooking and other arrangements such as decoration, preparing games, music, and songs.

### Could you describe some of the games you played?

The fruit eating competition is an enjoyable game because it is easy and very funny. It requires two or more participants to play. Watermelon, jicama, or other fruits will be provided to contestants. Then, they need to eat those fruits very quickly without using their hands. Whoever finishes first is the winner.

### What about Vai Khhorm?

*Vai Khhorm* (Breaking Pot) is a very popular traditional game played during Khmer New Year. Players need to prepare *khhorm* (pots): they put powder and candies in the pots, and then the pots are hung over our heads, making sure players can reach them using baseball bats. Players are blindfolded, spun around a few times, and then the competition starts. Surrounding people shout instructions: some to confuse players, some to help them break the pots and win!

*March 31, 2019*

A Busy Sunday

Oh! My very busy Sunday, but it was [such an] interesting day. In the morning, I had to join a meeting with my high school alumnae association. I was so happy to see them, especially my best friends. We talked about our high school's problems and how to help it. At the end of the meeting, I got good news, which is in May all alumnae students celebrate a party at school, and we also have four agendas that are going to focus on teaching and helping students to make decisions [for] after [they] graduate high school. I can't wait for that day. After [we] finished the meeting, I and my friends went to my rent house which is not near there. We had a great lunch together. I didn't want to leave there, but at 2:00 p.m. I had a leadership seminar at dorm. It was rush hour.

On this Sunday, the speaker is from the U.S. Embassy in Phnom Penh. She's [such an] amazing woman. All her words were very clear and awesome. I learned a lot from her that inspired me to keep going and fighting for my life. I will do what I want to be. It is real, not dreaming, so I will try my best.

✳ ✳ ✳

*April 1, 2019*

Today I got up at 7:15 in the morning. I was still on the bed. Oh! It was nearly time to go to school. I hurried to prepare something before going to school. It was a new term day in level five and I was a bit late for school, but it's okay. I was very happy to see my classmates again, and also delighted to study with new teachers. They are friendly and funny with a bit serious behavior. I like to study with them.

✳ ✳ ✳

*April 3, 2019*

After I finished class, I felt unhappy today. I don't know why? At college we had celebrated Songkran [Cambodian New Year] that made everyone look so happy.

I didn't talk a lot today, just thought about how my life is going to be. I had many tasks to do and I was worried about life and felt a bit down. I need some place to RELAX. I wish I was a child, that I could play. I miss my childhood. Life in university is not as easy as I thought. It requires a lot of responsibilities and a strong commitment.

Raksa, keep going girl!

✳ ✳ ✳

*April 6, 2019*

Unforgettable Songkran, Harpswell Day

Today, I got up so late because last night I had to prepare the decorations with the team for our Songkran day, so I went to bed at 1:45 a.m. However, today was a really amazing day for me. We continued to decorate our places, trees, and anywhere that we went. In the end, the decorations were wonderful. During the day, along with some other sisters, I also prepared food before it was cooked. I was a bit tired, but I really enjoyed doing it. In the evening, after everything was prepared, it was time to take photos, and some sisters who are Harpswell alumnae students attended. After that, we had a special dinner and it was so interesting. After dinner, we had popular Khmer games to play, such as answer the questions, fruit competition, Vai Khhorm and dancing. We had an awesome time together, having fun and strengthening our sisterhood. I spent a whole day with lovely sisters. I had a great time with them and they made me feel as warm as I am with my family.

Thanks, God, for giving me a very good opportunity.

*Thank you to the Harpswell Foundation for connecting me with Raksa.*

# Ruksar

**17**
years old

Lucknow, India

**Tell us about your family. What do your parents do?**

My father is a laborer. He also does some work as a carpenter in Delhi in someone else's shop. Ammi [Mother] sews clothes when orders come. That is how she pays our school fees. We have a very small family.

**Are you in school? Do you have a job?**

When I don't go to school, I do all the housework and also help with the sewing.

**Tell us about your friends.**

I feel very happy when I hang out with my friends Junaib, Faiza, Safiya, Sahil, Saba.

## "When I don't go to school, I do all the housework and also help with the sewing."

**RUKSAR IS A** seventeen-year-old girl who lives in a slum in Lucknow, a medium-sized city in India. Slums are crowded city neighborhoods where the inhabitants are often some of the poorest, and their homes can lack solid foundations and formal sanitation systems. Ruksar lives at home with her four siblings and her parents—her father is a daily wage-laborer (which generally involves manual labor, not office work), and her mother is a seamstress.

Ruksar's diary entries read more like a meticulous journal: she chronicles what she did and how she felt at different moments, with timestamps. Her accurate accounting of her hours paints a picture of days filled with schoolwork, teaching younger children, fasting for Ramadan (a Muslim holy month), and ever-relatable frustration when her mother won't let her join her friends at one of their houses. While Ruksar's parents are at work, she is often expected to be responsible for and take care of her younger siblings. ◊

Lucknow,
India

**THE DAYS RUKSAR** describes all exist within a broader context of what life in India is like for girls and young women. Since 2012, when the gang rape of a college student in Delhi made international headlines and sparked outrage, news from India has painted a dark and troubling picture of their lives.

Widespread violence against women and girls can have an impact on girls' daily lives. One study found that less than half of the girls living in cities in India said they could go out to meet friends, because of safety concerns.[89] The same study found that a significant percentage of girls in the country felt unsafe taking public transportation, going to the movies, or going out to play.

In this country of one billion people, statistics about the types of violence girls and women face are staggering. About 39,000 rapes were reported to police in 2016, more than 19,000 of those involving children.[90] And one study found only one percent of sexual assaults are reported, because women are afraid to go to police.[91]

But this isn't the only type of violence women and girls in the country are likely to face. According to one study, there are 21 million "unwanted" girls in the country—girls whose parents wanted sons, not daughters. These girls will likely have fewer educational opportunities and poorer nutrition than their brothers.[92]

The same study found that there are a total of 63 million "missing" women in the entire population of India. This number includes the two million each year who don't literally go missing, but who instead face neglect and disease, as well as female fetuses that are aborted because of a preference for boys over girls.[93] ◊

*Translated from Hindi*

*March 27, 2019*

7 a.m.—I woke up and made breakfast. I have a meeting in the school today so I have to finish all my work early.

9:30 a.m.—I have cooked the food and am now preparing for the meeting. People from outside are going to come so I am a little nervous but also excited as they will be good people.

10 a.m.—Now I am going to get the kids and go for the meeting.

1 p.m.—I am back home. I really enjoyed meeting those people and they did as well they said. I also felt a little bad as some of the children could not speak but doesn't matter. Now I am going to go eat.

2 p.m.—I am taking 4 children to the school to get their admission forms and get them admitted to school.

2:30 p.m.—We could not get the admission forms. They have called us [back on] Friday. I will go later with the kids. Today my mom has gone to the village. I am missing her.

3 p.m.—Going to study now.

4:30 p.m.—I am done studying for today. I was supposed to go to a friend's house. They have a dinner at their place. All my friends are there. I could not go as Ammi [Mother] didn't let me. I am feeling very bad and am crying.

7 p.m.—Going to teach the kids.

9 p.m.—The kids have left. I am going to cook food.

10:20 p.m.—Going to eat dinner.

11 p.m.—Going to sleep. I am still crying.

⁎ ⁎ ⁎

*April 2, 2019*

Today I woke up at 5 a.m. I have to do all the work early today as I have to make papad [a thin crispy food] later, so going to start cooking.

8:30 a.m.—Food is ready, I will go make papad.

11 a.m.—The papad are ready so I will go to work for a while.

12 noon—Going to teach for a while.

1:30 p.m.—Going to serve food now.

2 p.m.—Going to wash clothes now.

3:10 p.m.—Clothes are washed. Going to study.

5 p.m.—I am done studying. My sister has washed the utensils. Going to cook dinner.

7 p.m.—The kids have come to study. A few guests are coming over later.

8:30 p.m.—I have let the kids go. The guests are here.

10 p.m.—The guests have left so I will eat now.

10:30 p.m.—There is a [religious] function here today. I am going there. The priest is here giving a speech. Women are seated in a separate section. Everyone is seated. Snacks are served.

3:15 a.m.—Now we are going home. Today we have to start fasting for Ramadan* so I will go make tea for myself as I cannot eat anything all day today. I am very sleepy.

4 p.m.—I am going to sleep. Goodbye.

⁕ ⁕ ⁕

*April 4, 2019*

8:30 p.m.—Have let the kids go after studying. Ammi is making the vegetable. I am cooking the rice and chapatti [a type of bread].

9:45 p.m.—Food is ready. I am going to clean. All the work is done.

10 p.m.—Just sitting for a bit.

10:10 p.m.—Going to eat food now. There was a fight in the neighborhood. A boy hit his mother and sister. He swore at the sister about some boy. He is threatening to get back at her tomorrow. The mother is challenging him, saying, "Let's see what you can do."

1:20 a.m.—Am going to sleep now. Ammi is angry and says I won't go to anyone's house now.

*Thank you to Girl Icon and the Milaan Foundation for connecting me with Ruksar.*

* Traditionally, during the month of Ramadan, Muslims around the world will fast every day from sunrise to sunset.

# Ruoxiao

18 years old

Kunming, Yunnan, China, and the United Kingdom

**What are your favorite subjects in school?**
Further maths

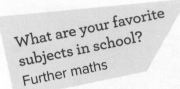

**What do you want to do when you grow up? What are your dreams?**
To become a physicist

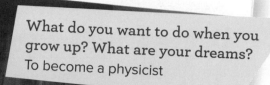

**How do you like to spend your time when you are not at school?**
Playing piano / erhu / guqin, Chinese painting, playing Rubik's Cube

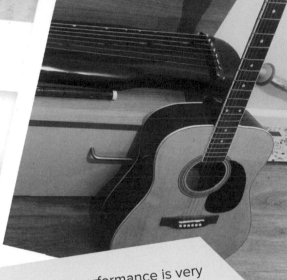

**Tell us about guqin.**
The sound of guqin is unique in that everyone's performance is very different. So, it really depends on an individual's style. This is why I love guqin, because there are no strict rules to follow. The sound of quqin is tiny. Some people say this is a musical instrument [that requires] listening to yourself, so there is a high demand for a quiet environment and a quiet inner heart. The school is quiet, but it is a place with too much worry; it's inevitable that weird notes pop up. I wish that there was a place [here] for this. It need not to be extremely beautiful with farms and lakes; I only want it to be clear, bright, and quiet—a place of understanding with heart.

# "When I was studying in China, I used to hate my unchanging life."

**"I LOVE MUSIC,** and I have a strong interest in classical music, hip-hop, and pop music," says Ruoxiao.

She's an eighteen-year-old girl from Kunming, in the Yunnan province of China. She now attends boarding school in the United Kingdom.

Ruoxiao pours her passion for music into a wide range of instruments: she plays erhu (a two-stringed instrument that is played with a bow), guqin (a seven-stringed instrument that is played by plucking), guitar, and piano. She also loves traditional Chinese opera—she finds magic in the stories and the songs— and she wishes more people appreciated it like she does.

When Ruoxiao is home in China, she lives with her parents. She's an only child, and her father is an engineer and her mother is a CIO, or chief information officer (a senior position in a company's technology department).

At school in England, Ruoxiao's favorite subject is math—she has fourteen math lessons a week, and she writes lyrically about the beauty and elegance she sees in the subject. She wants to be a physicist when she grows up.

Despite her enthusiasm for her schoolwork and music, Ruoxiao also describes how loneliness and homesickness settled in after the newness of pursuing her dreams and

Kumming,
Yunnan, China

United
Kingdom

living on another continent slowly wore off.

"Maybe because I am still young, maybe it's the effect of the law of diminishing marginal utility, an economics term," she writes. "New things always make me excited. Although I'm homesick, I never regret the decisions I have made." ◊

**FOR THE LAST FEW DECADES,** news stories about the lives of women and girls in China have often been linked to the country's one-child policy. This law, which was in place from 1979 to the end of 2015, prohibited families from having more than one child.[94] The exception was in the countryside, where families were allowed to have a second child if their first child was a girl or a disabled boy.

The one-child policy contributed to a vast gender imbalance in China, since many families preferred having a son to a daughter. Of the 1.4 billion people in China, there are 34 million more males than females[95]—about 120 boys for every 100 girls.[96]

This policy also affected what life looked like for girls. It often meant that "girls born in the city, because of lack of competition from brothers, have received unprecedented education opportunities by their families," according to Dr. Kailing Xie, who studies gender in contemporary China. In the countryside, however, "girls were hidden or neglected by families to have a son," she explained.

These are just some of the far-reaching impacts of the country's one-child policy. It has also affected the economy: housing prices and savings rates have soared, and there has been more trafficking (forced movement of people) of brides.[97] ◊

*Translated from Mandarin*

When I was studying in China, I used to hate my unchanging life and that I could see what my life would be in the next ten years: I would attend a second-rate university, get second-rate work, and then be a good wife and mother, playing mahjong with neighbors. So at that time my dream was to live abroad. The many possibilities there inspired me to pursue the beauty of life.

I have been in the UK for three years, and my dream now is to go back home. Returning to Kunming and enjoying a bowl of rice noodles seems to be the ultimate goal of three months of hard work.

Nonetheless, I don't regret my choice to go to the UK. It may be tasteless to eat rice noodles for three months straight. But without eating once I miss it so much. Perhaps people in itself are a contradiction, hating what you already have and always dreaming for the best.

Maybe because I'm still young, maybe it's the effect of the law of diminishing marginal utility, an economics term. New things always make me excited. Although I'm homesick, I never regret the decisions I have made.

※　※　※

The Yunnan Provincial Theatre is a place I usually go. Next to the Mabi chicken square, the tickets for the theater are very cheap. The front row only costs 40 RMB, and the rest are even cheaper—only 20 RMB per ticket. The audience in the theater is as I expected—only the elderly and their grandchildren. When the actor appeared, the old men always applaud . . . the timing was spot on, and not even one second behind. Shouting is a form of art.

The twists and turns of the story and slow tempo make the children bored. Every time I enter the theater, I am shocked by how fast this puts children to sleep, as if they are singing on the stage. The children simply can't wake up from their dreams.

Some people say that no one is watching the opera because of the lack of new stories and new ideas. It is necessary to adapt the old dramas and inject fresh blood. However, my personal perception is that it's adventurous to write ancient events with modern people's thoughts. To view the drama from another angle, it's necessary to have a deep understanding of an era and historical figures. You simply cannot rush it, it will take time to get used to it.

Chinese society is experiencing an unprecedented economic growth. Today, most people are chasing fame and fortune, but [society] lacks people who are willing to slow down to appreciate life. They fear that even if they stop for a second, wealth can slip from their fingers.

It is difficult for Chinese traditional opera to be accepted by the public in such an environment. It's a shame for the remaining few who wish to inherit this art, but I firmly believe that if there is still someone in the world who likes this drama, then this drama can exist.

✳ ✳ ✳

Our school has 14 math lessons in the week. There are four sessions on both Monday and Wednesday. A-level math and higher maths are boring: there are a lot of repetitions and a lack of new questions. Students seem to be able to get a high score as long as they take their time. These questions are exactly the opposite reason of why I love mathematics. Mathematics should be more logical, and more challenging, like philosophy, of deducing one thing from another . . . Mathematics is a language that needs communication. Communication makes mathematicians avoid many basic mistakes.

I like mathematics. I benefited from my four math teachers. My math teacher in elementary school made me realize that mathematics is interesting. My tutors gave me a certain degree of precision, so that I have the confidence to learn mathematics. My junior high school teacher let me know that math problems can be answered from multiple angles. My high school teacher led me to discover that mathematics is a language, a game for bored people, and a key to all fields. I learned the romance of Descartes today, $r = a(1+\cos)$; I feel ecstatic.

✳ ✳ ✳

It's not surprising that days become repetitive when you come to the UK alone to study, but the boredom and loneliness gave me a lot more time to think, read, and try new things. The author Mr. Wang Zengqi gives me a lot of inspiration in his books. For example, today, the topic of how to write a short story piqued my interest. His description of writing multiple novels spoke to me; that breathless, full-hearted creation process is extremely short, putting pen to paper in the morning and completing the whole thing by night time, the author fully immersed and unconscious to the passing of time.

The idea that writing must be done with a pen limits me and inevitably forces me into the constraints of language. Trying to find profound meaning in an ordinary life is difficult, but I also hesitated to get closer to the lives of the ordinary people, as if making them say something bad or do something bad in the story was some great sin. And so the creation process of my first short story was an unhappy one. Although I didn't end up completing the story, I experienced the process from sunrise to sunset. I guess the thing I felt most guilty about then was that I didn't revise [study] my schoolwork for that day.

# Ruqaya

**16** years old

Baghdad, Iraq

**Tell us about your family.**
My father is an engineer and my mother is not working now, but she worked in the past.

**What do you want to do after school?**
I want to study journalism and build an orphanage and a home for the elderly.

**Tell us a little about your friends.**
I have many friends always. I am that girl that everyone loves for no reason. I have a friend named Duha and I have Zainab. We quarrel all the time but love each other.

# "I have many friends always, I am that girl that everyone loves for no reason."

Baghdad, Iraq

**WHAT IS IT LIKE** to grow up in a country that has been defined by conflict your entire lifetime?

Ruqaya, a teenage girl who loves to read and spend time with her friends and family, shows us a little glimpse of life in Baghdad, the capital of Iraq, in her diary entries.

The Iraq we see through Ruqaya's eyes is one of shopping malls, exams at school, and long chats about marriage and life with friends. This is pointedly different from the Iraq we see in the news: for the last two decades, Iraq has mostly made headlines for war and bloodshed[98]—first for the fighting that followed the U.S. and UK's invasion of Iraq in 2003, and then because of the rise of the Islamic State in parts of the country.

But Ruqaya's daily life in Baghdad, where she lives with her parents, her brothers, and her aunts, is not dominated by conflict. She writes about reading novels, studying for exams, and spending time with her many friends. "We argue all the time but we love each other." ◊

186

**RUQAYA WRITES OFTEN** about her friends, teenagers like her, many of whom are married. When I asked her about this, she said, "Most of my friends marry at a young age but I will not marry until I finish my studies."

Unlike many of her friends' parents, Ruqaya's parents encourage her to pursue her education, and she wants to wait to marry until she's older. She wants to focus on school for now, and she wants to be a computer engineer (or a journalist—she gives me different answers each time I ask her this question). She's seen her friends get married and get pregnant in their teenage years, and be forced to drop out of school.

This, unfortunately, isn't atypical. Almost one quarter of girls in Iraq marry before they turn eighteen, according to Girls Not Brides, an international organization that works to prevent child marriage around the world.[99] And it's not just Iraq. Child marriages occur across cultures and continents—from the United States to Algeria to Australia.

"Child marriage usually spells the end to a girl's education. She is usually expected to leave school and to swap children's activities like playing for grown-up responsibilities like cooking and cleaning. Once she is out of school, it is very hard to go back," says Dr. Rachel Yates, Interim Executive Director of Girls Not Brides. "Without a school education, a girl will struggle to get a well-paid job in the future. Child marriage typically traps her in low-paid or informal work, making it hard for her to support her family."

There are many reasons why teenage girls in different cultures and communities might be married. An underlying reason is gender inequality.

"In many parts of the world, a boy is seen as a future earner, somebody who should be educated so that he can grow up to support the whole family. His sister, by contrast, is expected to become a wife and mother," explains Yates. "Because of this, many families see educating their daughters as a waste of money, and will choose to spend their limited money on keeping boys in school while marrying their daughters off young."

Poverty, natural disasters, and conflict are some of the other reasons that families might force their teenage daughters to marry. ◊

*Some of Ruqaya's diary entries were translated from Arabic to English, others were written in English. When I first explained the project to Ruqaya, instead of diary entries, she took to texting me at the end of each day about her day—which is why these entries might be shorter than others in the book, and her photos often look like cell phone selfies.*

*May 8*

I woke up at seven in the morning. I had a whole set of tasks, and I had to go to school to bring important papers from school. I met my friends there; we are now on vacation. I have a bigger friend than me, and I have known her for five years. She told me about the story of her sister's harassment. I told her to tell her mother but she refused because she was scared of her family because they would not believe her sister. She married at the age of 14 (I mean her sister). I was frustrated because I could not help her.

✳ ✳ ✳

*May 9*

I woke up at 8 a.m. and arranged the house and then I studied for the exam. When I got back at 12 noon, I prayed. When I finished praying, I received a message from an old friend that she was pregnant. She is 18 years old and married when she was 15 years old. Happy because I trust that she will be able to complete her studies and pregnancy together. When it became at 5 p.m., my mother and I went to buy some necessities for the house and when I returned from the outside we attended to the food and then I washed dishes and then completed all my duties.

*May 10*

I woke up at 9 a.m. I had no work and wanted this day to rest only. I did nothing but take care of myself, rest after a very long and tiring week. I read my favorite novels and I spent the day without doing anything except comfort and played my favorite game and I read my favorite books and at 5 p.m. I went out with my brother and mother to get some fresh air and on our return we ate.

✳ ✳ ✳

*May 15*

I woke up at 7 a.m. I arranged my room and then I had a shower. I had a date to go out with my friends to the mall. We went out at 9 a.m. We met and went out together. We arrived at the mall at 10 a.m. I was happy and I had a beautiful trip with my friends. We did some shopping for clothes and other things and I went to the library, I always get books . . . then we went to the Baghdadi Museum. We got acquainted with some of the histories of ancient Iraq, we toured a lot . . . then returned home. It was a day of pleasure, I am very tired.

*Thank you to Mercy Hands for connecting me with Ruqaya.*

# Sattigul

## 16
### years old

Ulaankhus, Mongolia

**Could you tell us about your eagle?**
Watching the eagle [named Akhyikh] always gives me courage and energy. He likes to eat his meals on my hand. When my father is not home, I always give him food.

**What are your favorite subjects?**
English and geography

**What are your hobbies?**
Playing chess, riding horses, and playing ball

> "Watching the eagle always gives me courage and energy. He likes to eat his meals on my hand. When my father is not home, I always give him food."

**"I LIKE TO LEARN** new things," says Sattigul. "In the future I would like to be an English translator. It is my dream."

Sattigul lives in the mountains of western Mongolia with her family. She is one of five siblings, and her family members are nomadic herders who move with the seasons. They move four times a year: In the winter and spring, they live in the valley of the mountains. In the summer and fall, they live in the steppe, or the grassland. With every season, they can move anywhere from twenty to more than one hundred miles.

In the summertime, her family makes their traditional ger dwellings, which are large round tents, near other herding families. Sattigul loves these months, because they have neighbors and she gets to play with other children.

But her family passes the winter months alone. The other nomadic families also have houses in the valley, but they are far from one another. "We

Ulaankhus,
Mongolia

cannot meet our neighbors and friends. We meet our friends only during school time," she explains.

Since her family is nomadic, Sattigul lives in a dormitory when school is in session, as do some of her siblings. Sattigul has been living in the dormitory since she was seven years old, and she says she sometimes misses home.

This is common, according to Lena Khazidolda, who runs Source of Steppe Nomads, an organization that provides education, health, development, and other programs for nomadic families in Mongolia.

Eagle hunting—where eagles help hunt for small animals—is part of the nomadic lifestyle. After hunting with an eagle for a few years, the hunter lets the eagle go and live in nature wherever it wants.

Sattigul's father has been an eagle hunter for 25 years, and Sattigul has grown up watching and learning from him. When she asked her father why they let the eagles go, he told her that "eagles must live free and happy in nature."

The nomads even have a celebration before freeing the eagles. Sattigul explains: "Before letting them fly far away, all hunters have a special party and tie white cotton to the eagles' leg, which is meant to wish them good luck." ◊

**SATTIGUL'S FAMILY ARE** nomadic herders—about one third of the population lives this traditional Mongolian lifestyle.[100] They have sheep and goats, and sometimes also yaks, horses, and camels. The families earn their living from their animals' products, such as wool, meat, and milk.

But slowly, this lifestyle is changing. In the last thirty years, more than 600,000 former herders have migrated to Ulaanbaatar, the country's capital.[101] One of the primary reasons for this is climate change—in the last seventy years, temperatures in Mongolia have risen three times faster than the world's average, and this has made it harder for herders and their animals to survive.

Climate change has made winters colder and summers hotter. In 2017, Mongolia had the hottest summer in about fifty years and faced a severe drought. Additionally, part of its land has turned into a desert. There now isn't enough grass for animals to survive the brutal winters, which are only getting harsher, as temperatures can reach 40 degrees below freezing.[102] ◊

*Translated from Mongolian*

*April 27, 2019*

Today is Saturday. I stayed at home. In the morning I got up at 8 a.m. and made a fire. I had breakfast.

After that, at 8:30 a.m., I helped my parents to forage for cattle and livestock. And after that, I came back home. Then I cleaned the dirt from the home. We had lunch at 11:30 a.m. Then my mother and I cooked some handmade bread. After, I went with my mother to the river to bring ice that will melt then be used for cooking.

I usually do both outside and inside household work. In the afternoon, I mostly help my dad and older brother take care of animals.

❋ ❋ ❋

*April 28, 2019*

I got up at 8 a.m. this morning, and I had breakfast. After that I foraged for the cattle and livestock. I had a lot of work to finish; I have no idea how I managed all of it. It was windy outside.

In the afternoon, I went to mountain area with my daddy, because we needed to transfer some household supplies to our autumn camp. On the way, we also let our eagle fly and have some food.

Watching the eagle always gives me courage and energy. I like to spend more time with my eagle.

*April 29, 2019*

Today I also got up at 8:00 a.m. After breakfast I went to my school. Our lessons start at 8:30 a.m. and go to 2:30 p.m. I like to learn and spend my time with my friends. After lessons, we went to the dormitory and had lunch together. I did my homework. Then I read a book in my free time. I like reading interesting books. Then I had dinner at 7:00 p.m. Today's weather was warm and clear.

*Thank you to Source of Steppe Nomads NGO for connecting me with Sattigul.*

# Shanai

## 18
### years old

### Tell us about your friends.

I have three and a half friends: Darljit, Hannah, Angel, and Yamali. Darljit I've known since 6th grade and we don't see each other often at all but we text almost every day, if not every day. She is probably my best friend because she knows my biggest thing is that I want to be listened to and feel heard and she is always there just for that. She's kind of like a yes-man, she's always supporting me and telling me how proud she is of me or happy she is for me, which I don't think I could've survived without. Hannah and I have been friends since sophomore year. I met Angel in an acting / social justice program that honestly felt like group therapy up until we finally put on a show. Yamali is the half because although I fully value her as a friend, she likes to keep her distance. We met in 6th grade—she, Darljit, and I were all friends and in the same classes. Yamali and I have hung out outside of school and I know her family, she's met some of mine, and to this day I go to her house sometimes because I know I'm always welcome.

### What do you like doing outside of school?

Outside of school, I love being in spaces to write and do open mics. And dance and DJ and chill and share my thoughts freely. I also love walking in the night; it makes me feel free and when no one else is out everything feels so still. I love looking at the sky and seeing stars or the moon. It feels beautiful. I also really love eating, anything with bread or carbs in general, that's the way to my heart.

### Who's your favorite author?

I'm going to college for creative writing with the aim to provide my readers with content that is not only entertaining but also thought-provoking. My favorite author is James Baldwin because his work does that so well. I just also want to be able to give even those who aren't avid readers a chance to appreciate the power of words and telling stories.

# "Writing is the only thing that allows me to be my true self. When I write, it's like my soul is speaking."

**THIS IS HOW** Shanai describes herself: "Shanai is a black girl from the Bronx."

But there's more, of course.

Shanai is one of seven siblings, although none share both parents with her. She has a rocky relationship with her mother, a payroll clerk for PATH, a transit system that runs between New Jersey and New York City; and she is close to her father.

"Family means a lot to me, especially because I used to live in a house of seven

and my family split up sometime after my fifth-grade graduation," Shanai says. "It broke my heart, and I'm still recovering."

Even though she now lives in Bayonne, New Jersey—right across the river from New York City—she grew up in the Bronx and claims the bustling and diverse NYC as her home. The city houses more than eight million people, including many who have lived there for generations and immigrants who have arrived from around the world. In fact,

Bayonne,
New Jersey,
United States
of America

as many as eight hundred languages are spoken in New York City.[103]

Shanai's favorite classes in school have always been those that involve writing. "Writing is the only thing that allows me to be my true self. When I write, it's like my soul is speaking," she says. "And because of that I'm going to college for creative writing with the aim to provide my readers with content that is not only entertaining but thought-provoking."

Her life is rich, busy, and diverse: in addition to attending school, she interns at a nonprofit, spends time with her friends, writes poetry, dances, DJs, goes to open mics . . . The list is long.

Shanai is fiercely bright, thoughtful, ambitious, and talented. And she has big dreams for what her life will hold. "My future is going to be filled with writing and children. I am going to be a bestselling author," she says definitively. ◊

**IN THE DIARY** entries she shared, Shanai writes a lot about a boy she likes: from falling for him to their breakup. When she first shared her diary entries with me, she was worried about writing so much about a boy. This is how girls and women are often portrayed in books, movies, and other pop culture—they are defined only or primarily in the context of boys and men who are their romantic interests. American cartoonist Alison Bechdel came up with a test to measure the impact of this phenomenon. For a film to pass the Bechdel test, it would have to have the following:

1. More than two women characters
2. Who talk to each other
3. About something other than a man.

Less than half of all movies that have won an Oscar for best picture pass the test.[104]

In this context, Shanai's concern makes sense—just because she writes about a boy, it doesn't mean that he is the only thing, or the defining thing, in her life. But their relationship was a big part of her life at the time, which is why she decided to share her thoughts about it.

In fact, according to Deborah Welsh, a professor of psychology at the University of Tennessee, Knoxville, who studies teenagers' and young adults' romantic relationships, our romantic relationships in our teenage years are an important way for us to understand ourselves. She says they serve a purpose that is "like holding up a mirror."

When Welsh studied how teens acted in relationships, she found that they saw themselves in their partner, "so it was like a mirror to say, 'Who am I? What kind of person am I?' " ◊

*October 19, 2018*

I feel really good right now & very loving.

I love my boyfriend.

He is so sweet.

His cheeks are so fat.

He kind of reminds me of a kid.

I love when he's sleeping.

I love when he's half asleep or just waking up. I love how his eyes look. I love his forehead. I love his widow's peak. I love that if I look @ him @ a certain angle I can see him how he looked as a kid.

When he was funny looking and ugly-cute.

Not ugly ugly. He's never been that. His face was just interesting and adorable. I miss my baby. I want to feel his warm hands. I want to see his eyes. His eyes panic when I'm not smiling. I love his smile; sometimes I smile just so I can see his. Sometimes I stare @ him not smiling and his smile fades and I watch it. It makes me so sad. I love it when he's smiling. I just wish I made him smile more. I don't think I am a very good girlfriend sometimes. I do want to go to therapy because there are a lot of things I seek out from Brian that he won't be able to satisfy me to the degree that I need and I know the person I really need to seek things from is myself. I love my boyfriend. I hope we do stay together, forever.

I hope college helps us grow individually but not apart. I hope we both stay faithful. I hope I stop having too many overwhelming thoughts at once. I just want to enjoy my baby. My sweet boy.

✳ ✳ ✳

*October 22 2018*

I'm scared I'm outgrowing my boyfriend. I love him like a mother loves her child, or should. He asked me if I thought I was losing feelings for him. And I said no because I didn't want to think so or say yes. And I said no because I didn't think so. And I still don't. I am scared I am outgrowing my boyfriend. I am scared I am not ready for his love. Or I am too much for his love. Or not enough for his love. I am scared I don't deserve his love. I'm in my thoughts about girls and females and the feeling that I am or could be missing out on something. I'm scared that these thoughts could be more than thoughts or want to be more than thoughts. I'm scared that in college we won't be able to grow individually and simultaneously so that we still love each other as much and more and are ready to be together when there's less constraints and circumstances. I'm scared that I want to stop this beautiful love in hopes of picking it back up later. I'm scared because I know things won't work like that. I'm scared I'm asking for too much. I'm scared that I'm going to lose what I love.

Why is this not enough?

*February 23, 2019*

This would've made 10 months if he didn't break up with me last night.

Is he still responsible for the breakup if I suggested it?

It's easy to just blame everything on myself. Being that I am depressed officially. You kind of just know. And I know talking bad about myself won't help me. Since I'm all I have after all.

I wish I could've been better @ explaining things. I wish I had a true lesson in Emotional Maturity 101. I learn as I go. Maybe that's why I'm getting better @ admitting when I'm wrong or trying to understand others' feelings.

I'm grateful for my family.

I love them very much.

I'm grateful for my body.

She may not have eaten

But she's still holding up. *

Such a sweet pretty girl. I love me. I love me. I love me. I love me. I love me. It's okay to be sad sometimes. It's okay, baby.

✳ ✳ ✳

*March 24, 2019*

Yoo OMG today was such a good day.

I hung out w/ Hannah and Darljit.

* Shanai sometimes writes lists of things she is grateful
for in her journal—the list in this entry is one of them.

203

Got some beautiful pics. We got great ice cream. The weather was cute we were cute. And that's the first thing I'm grateful for because I haven't had an all around good celebration of my bday inna min. And this was really reassuring. That all things shall pass.

2nd I'll give to Tasha. I am so grateful I get to not only be out of my crib this weekend but still shower / do my hair / live laugh and be loved.

3rd is Jhanique.

I might be downplaying how much I like her? IDK. I don't want to get attached I'm let her be my girl but like IDK I don't want to pull a Brian. I don't think I am anyway. I mean we'll see I guess.

But I'm not a scumbag like some people . . . Idk what I'm downplaying or upplaying or playing but I'm glad we're being us. I just want things to be alright.

4th Daddy

I'm grateful daddy supports me though he can't be physically present. He frets over my emotions, health, and financial situations. I'm very appreciative of him.

5. Me

I'm grateful I am beginning to make good decisions. And stick to my routines and just be a better overall me.

I am so grateful for that.

I love you, Shanai.

I love you.

I love you.

You're amazing.

Keep it up, baby.

# Sofia

18 years old

Panama City, Panama

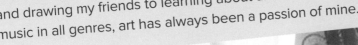

## What are some things you like to do outside of school?

I've shown an interest in art my whole life. From painting the walls of my room and drawing my friends to learning about art theory and listening to alternative music in all genres, art has always been a passion of mine.

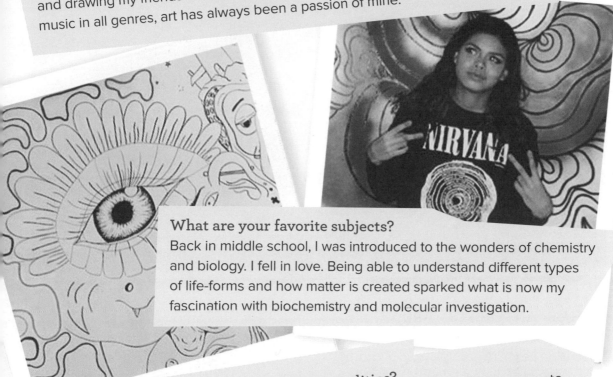

## What are your favorite subjects?

Back in middle school, I was introduced to the wonders of chemistry and biology. I fell in love. Being able to understand different types of life-forms and how matter is created sparked what is now my fascination with biochemistry and molecular investigation.

## Could you tell us more about your interest in politics?

If a few years back, someone would've told me that I was going to be very passionate about human rights, social issues, and even go as far as to be the president of my school's debate club—and on top of that, getting the chance to present a draft bill in congress with several of my pro-education partners . . . I'd NEVER have believed it.

As someone who is concerned for her country's future, I got involved with organizations and movements that try to tackle the current status quo through improving our educational system. Also, one of my most recent projects is the Observatorio Contra el Acoso Callejero (Observatory Against Street Harassment). Our goal is to show the harmful effects of sexual harassment and assault in public spaces so that our politicians take this topic seriously. This initiative was born from personal experiences shared among many women, the need to solve this problem and the opportunity to join an international collective of organizations that were interested in including Panama in the statistics of the "Latina reality."

**SOFIA'S INTERESTS ARE** diverse: art, science, and politics. She's painted murals on her bedroom walls, is planning to study biomedicine in college, and is a passionate activist who has presented a draft bill to Panama's government.

She was born in Costa Rica, but she grew up and lives in Panama City with her parents and two younger sisters. Her mother's side of the family is Costa Rican, her father's side Panamanian, and she has Filipino roots as well. Her parents are both professionals with managerial jobs, her father at an insurance company and her mother at an electricity company. Sofia is planning to study biological sciences and hopes to do research in the "pharmaceutical industry and all around the health care system."

"Living in Panama as a young woman is hard to describe," says Sofia. "Latino culture is very traditional, leaning towards religious beliefs. Society sometimes feels harsh on women as a whole. But Panama has a very globalized city. We are known for being a meeting point among countries and constantly referred to as a *crisol de razas* (melting pot). Meaning, many cultures have contributed to the Panamanian way of thinking and living."

She is committed to politics and activism, and she writes both about her day-to-day routines and the political causes she cares deeply about. ◊

"As someone who is concerned for her country's future, I got involved with organizations and movements that try to tackle the current status quo through improving our educational system."

Panama City,
Panama

**IN ONE OF** her diary entries, Sofia writes about a day spent cleaning up the beach. She shares her worries about the impact of discarded plastic on the oceans and on Panama's biodiversity (the variety of plant and animal life that lives and grows there). The country is home to more than 10,000 types of plants, 250 species of mammals, and 970 species of birds.[105]

Sofia has good reason for concern. According to some reports, if people around the world don't make significant changes, there could be more plastic than fish in our oceans by 2050.[106] And Sofia lives in a part of the world that experts say is highly vulnerable to the impacts of climate change.[107] Central America, a region with long coastlines and lowlands situated between two oceans, regularly deals with droughts, flooding, and cyclones.[108]

Sofia's concern for the environment is something we see not just in Central America, but also among her peers around the world. Teenage activists have taken the megaphone and are speaking up about the effect of human actions on the environment. It only makes sense: teens will inherit the earth and will live through the impact of today's actions. ◊

*Wednesday, April 10, 2019*

Diary:

Today I had a full scheduled day. I don't enjoy feeling like I'm doing the exact same thing every day, so I try to focus on my work individually to prevent getting overwhelmed. Today I woke up at 6 a.m., got ready and had breakfast. Then I rushed to my nearest metro station to start my day. The metro train public transportation is quite new, but it has improved many Panamanian lifestyles. From there I usually walk to my destination. With this said, some Panamanian streets don't have sidewalks, and if they do they're quite small. I think this is one of the reasons why people don't prefer walking; also because the weather makes it difficult sometimes. We say we have two seasons: hot summer and rainy summer. Humidity is always present too. I have to admit that I don't mind it, I enjoy [being] out in the sun. However, rain is a whole different story. Luckily, these past few days it's been very nice and windy so I've had no problem running errands.

I went to my grandpa's house because he lives closer to downtown. We used to live there when we first moved from Costa Rica to Panama so it feels like a second home. The area where he lives is called La Loceria. This place is next to El Dorado, which is known as a small "Chinatown." Many Chinese descendant families have their businesses in El Dorado and also live here. Establishments such as restaurants, dry cleaners, and even a casino make up this place. I have a special connection with this neighborhood because I grew up next to it. The school I graduated from is Chinese-Panamanian and is also in this area. From elementary to high school, I grew up learning Mandarin Chinese and Taiwanese culture. It is very ironic because my family has a Filipino descendance, so I look Asian to some people plus I speak Mandarin Chinese and understand the culture. You could imagine how much of an ethnic enigma I may seem for those who don't know me that well.

After that I went to the gym as usual. What a busy day!

Love, Sof

✳ ✳ ✳

*Saturday, April 20, 2019*

Diary:

Panama is celebrating Holy Week* and today me and my friends are going to the beach. Every year, companies and schools will give a couple of days off to their workers and students because of the holiday. Even though not everyone commemorates this religious festivity, we have a Catholic background as a society, and a small vacation never killed nobody. We woke up early and hit the road. My friend's dog, Henry, came with us because we had no other option than to bring him. He was the first one to jump in the car.

Arriving to a beach was quite the adventure. We are surrounded by the sea; literally Panama meets both the Atlantic and

* Holy Week is the week leading up to Easter, including Maundy Thursday, Good Friday, and Easter Sunday. These holidays are observed in Panama—a majority of the country's population is Catholic—and include religious services and celebrations.

Pacific Ocean, but there are a lot of polluted beaches. Coronado Beach was our final destination. I have to admit that me and my friends spent most of the trip taking pictures, but nonetheless we had a lot of fun. Going to the beach is one of my favorite things to do so it is very heartbreaking to see them get contaminated. I wish our government focused more on nature's conservation than on industrialization. Few countries possess our biodiversity and I think we aren't aware of how lucky we are.

Before leaving, my friend's mom decided to clean up the area a bit. Me and friends helped her by picking up all the beer cans, plastic bags, candy wraps, plastic containers, and any other piece of trash we could find. People were staring at us but we didn't care. Then we sat on the seashore, where the waves break, close enough just to get our feet wet while we watched the sunset. Listening to Señor Loop, a regional band, we talked a lot about our friendship and everything that was going on in our lives. In a few months, each one of us is going to be in a different continent and none of us is sure when we are going to reunite. Social media came up in the conversation. It's funny how we are more connected than ever in the history of humanity but somehow friendships and relationships seem to be more fragile. I hope time treats us good and in the future we're able to look back to all the moments we shared as friends, together.

Love, Sof

# Sophie

## 17
### years old

St. Louis, Missouri, United States of America

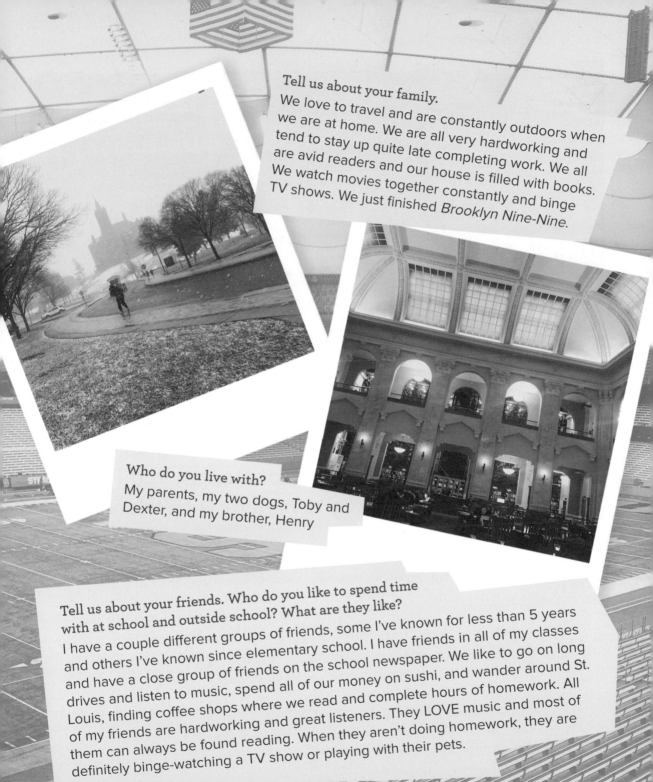

**Tell us about your family.**
We love to travel and are constantly outdoors when we are at home. We are all very hardworking and tend to stay up quite late completing work. We all are avid readers and our house is filled with books. We watch movies together constantly and binge TV shows. We just finished *Brooklyn Nine-Nine*.

**Who do you live with?**
My parents, my two dogs, Toby and Dexter, and my brother, Henry

**Tell us about your friends. Who do you like to spend time with at school and outside school? What are they like?**
I have a couple different groups of friends, some I've known for less than 5 years and others I've known since elementary school. I have friends in all of my classes and have a close group of friends on the school newspaper. We like to go on long drives and listen to music, spend all of our money on sushi, and wander around St. Louis, finding coffee shops where we read and complete hours of homework. All of my friends are hardworking and great listeners. They LOVE music and most of them can always be found reading. When they aren't doing homework, they are definitely binge-watching a TV show or playing with their pets.

"When I'm not at school, I'm most likely in bed reading, in comfy clothes and drinking a cup of tea. I hang out with friends constantly, and I go on drives often, either by myself or with friends."

**IN THE SPRING** of 2019, Sophie and her mother took a road trip through the northeastern United States to visit colleges. For Sophie, a high school student living in a suburb of St. Louis, Missouri, the trip was a chance to explore what her future could look like.

She took tours of universities, sat in on classes, and attended presentations. The trip was also incredibly scenic, and included visits to colleges that reminded Sophie of Hogwarts, the castle from the Harry Potter series. "We saw quaint farms and small towns. Everything was ensconced in a layer of snow, which made the drive even more peaceful," she says.

Sophie participated in the original "Girlhood Around the World" series that appeared in *The Lily* in 2018, and I've also included entries from that summer, when anticipation of the school year ahead and the anxiety of applying to college weighed heavily on

216

St. Louis, Missouri,
United States of America

her. A few months later, in the spring of 2019, she shared entries from the week when she was visiting colleges with journalism programs and sitting in on classes, taking the ACT (a standardized test for college admissions), and beginning to imagine what her future could look like.

Sophie's a voracious reader who has grown up in a home full of books and wants to be a journalist when she grows up. She was actively thinking about the future when she wrote these entries, and college applications feature frequently in her writing. ◊

**IN ADDITION TO** to the excitement of figuring out her future, Sophie also writes about stress, anxiety, and her struggles with mental health. Academics and college applications weigh on her, but she's found ways to cope.

"When I'm not at school, I'm most likely in bed reading, in comfy clothes and drinking a cup of tea. I hang out with friends constantly, and I go on drives often, either by myself or with friends," she says. "I spend lots of time with my pets and my family and I travel often, which is a great escape, especially when my mental health isn't doing so well."

Sophie isn't alone in this. Mental health is a significant concern for teens across the country. A staggering 70 percent of teens in the United States said they saw anxiety and depression as a major problem for their peers.[109]

About one in five American children have a diagnosable mental, emotional, or behavioral disorder, according to the Centers for Disease Control and Prevention.[110] And this experience is particularly gendered: according to one 2017 study, 36 percent of teenage girls in the U.S. experience depression, compared to about 13 percent of teenage boys.[111]

In the U.S., teens report facing many stressors: from the pressure to do well in school to the pressure to look good.[112] ◊

*July 21, 2018*

Normally when I spend time with family, I feel isolated and alone, and gradually become a closed-off version of myself. But with these cousins, the exact opposite happens. I always feel lighter and happier with them. Even though Grace was at her camp most of the day, I still had fun with my other cousin, Thomas, her brother. My brother, Thomas, and I walked around the Illinois State campus, our laughter a constant echo. I liked the campus, but am not considering going there. I'll be starting my junior year of high school, so college is now looming in the distance. I'm excited for change, but scared out of my mind as well.

When we got back to the hotel, I got some snacks and Uno, and headed down to the lobby where I played card games for a couple hours with Thomas and my brother. When the clock was nearing 11 p.m., we became instantly slaphappy and everything was superbly funny. I cannot begin to explain the immense joy I feel around them, but I definitely know I am a better version of myself when I'm in their company. We bring out the best in each other, something I hold dear to my heart.

The one word I can use to describe today would be joy, a word not constantly seen in my everyday life. Despite all the good things in my life, I have many struggles, which can get the best of me. I've grappled with different mental illnesses since I was in elementary school. Now I'm a junior and still struggling. Some days are darker than others. That's why I'm glad I have constants in my life such as my family to keep me grounded and happy.

✳ ✳ ✳

*July 23, 2018*

I cleaned my room, did some laundry, and read more of my book. I really like cleaning. It calms me and every thought rushes from my head whenever I organize things. I guess that happens because no matter how chaotic my life is, cleaning makes me feel in control.

My plan for the rest of the day is to brush both of my dogs because they are shedding like crazy right now and then take them to the dog park. I'll bring my book and read while they run around. I highly recommend reading at dog parks. It's so relaxing because if you're in the middle of a boring scene and need a break, looking at all the dogs running around is perfect.

Summer is slowly ending and I'm excited but scared. I have to take the ACT this year and begin searching for colleges. I know that I want to be a journalist and I'm already working toward that goal by being a features writer on my school's newspaper. I'm reading so many books so I can take in a plethora of writing styles and hopefully find mine in the process.

I'm looking forward to falling back into the routine of school and the constant work, even if it feels like I'm drowning in it at times. I had a pretty tough last school year, so I hope this school year is better.

✳ ✳ ✳

*March 18, 2019*

Today was a busy day to say the least. I'm currently on a college road trip with my mom, and we're visiting 4 colleges known for their journalism programs.

Today, I visited Syracuse and fell in love with the school. It had the perfect mix of old and modern architecture, some of the buildings looked as though they had been taken right out of the Harry Potter books, which was actually a requirement I had for the college I want to go to. We started our day at Syracuse with a presentation from a current science professor. The slides contained great information about the school and we also watched a video showcasing the school's goals for its students, as well as many on-campus activities students can participate in.

After the presentation, tour guides broke up our group of about 90 people into even sections for a campus tour. We got to see through the eyes of two energetic students who both were majoring in journalism. We saw various buildings that house schools within the university (i.e. math, science), two libraries, a dining hall, dorm room, sports dome, church, and the journalism building.

Everything is state of the art, and I was blown away by how cozy everything felt. Syracuse has a lot to offer and I know I will definitely be applying :)

✳ ✳ ✳

*April 2, 2019*

It's been a week since I've come back from school and today we took the ACT. I didn't study because this was my first time taking it, so I wanted to see how I would do with no preparation. I took the practice ACT in September and did okay on it, so I'm slightly worried about my score. Overall, the test went fine. I love English so the reading section was actually kind of fun and I enjoyed doing the grammar. Math is my weakest subject so I don't feel confident about that section and science was just okay. I was exhausted after the test, but I went out to lunch with a group of my close friends because we were celebrating the 3rd year of us being friends. We had a lot of fun and it was nice catching up with all of them. After lunch, I went home and did about 6 hours of homework, which was tough. I got everything done though, so I managed to be productive despite being tired from the stress of my day.

# Varvara

## 18
### years old

Saransk, Russia

### Tell us about your friends.

As for friends, recently I lost faith in the existence of female friendship. All those whom I have called my friends for a long time either betrayed me or simply left my life. The latest betrayal was especially painful, as it was probably the most unexpected. Perhaps there is only one person who allows me not to lose hope. This is Ksenia. She is close to me in spirit, and the nature of our beauty is similar (I mean that we do not look like typical Instagram girls). She is smart and intelligent, bright and bold, a go-getter and freedom-loving, and she also has a delicate and sensitive soul.

### Tell us about Max.

I don't know if this is love or just coincidence, but thanks largely to him I am now writing this text here. For the most part, it was for his sake that I stayed in my hometown, forgoing my dream of studying in the capital. I wanted a family, although I had previously been disgusted by the thought that I would be sharing a bed and worldview with someone. He taught me a lot and still keeps pulling me up when I'm drowning. Now our relationship is more like friendship.

### What do you want to do when you grow up?

Since the ninth grade, I knew that I wanted to connect my life with journalism. For 17 years, I worked hard and long to achieve all my goals, but I had overestimated my potential, my body could not stand it, and I fell down from a huge height of the self-made Olympus. Now I am studying philology in my native city. And I'm happy! The only thing that upsets me is that I have given up blogging on Instagram and I have generally stopped writing.

"I used to count the minutes when I leave this ad nauseam calm province, but now I understand that life is not only an eternal race for unattainable ideals and round-the-clock revelry, but also a time of contemplation and reflection."

**VARVARA IS A** college student studying philology, which is the study of the history of language, especially in written texts. She's eloquent and thoughtful, and she writes lyrically about the pace of life in her town, about the books she reads, and about the ways she hopes her life will unfold.

"I used to count the minutes when I leave this ad nauseam calm province, but now I understand that life is not only an eternal race for unattainable ideals and round-the-clock revelry, but also a time of contemplation and reflection," she says. "That is why in old age I would not want to suffocate in the

Saransk,
Russia

megalopolis, but I would like to live my life in the same quiet place where there are ducks in the tiny pond in the park." Now, she has exchanged her dream of a life in Moscow for an apartment with twenty-three-year-old Max, a man she loves, in the city (she likes to call it her "village") of Saransk.

Varvara left home when she and her mother were fighting often, but now, she says, "I am grateful to fate for having found a best friend in my mom."

Varvara grew up with two strong women as role models, and writes with admiration about both her mother and sister, who are hardworking and tough. "My sister evokes admiration: she did not break, living in hell, went to Moscow, worked there, and sent money to us when she herself only had enough to either eat or to take the bus home," she explains.

Varvara's mother also endured in-credibly trying circumstances.

"What my mom did was truly a feat. Taking care of my sister (11 years older than me) and me, when my father left her during pregnancy, she spared no effort, working at three places," she says. ◊

**VARVARA ALSO WRITES** about her experience with anorexia.

"For five years now, I have been actively resisting with various manifestations of self-hatred: the terrible path of anorexia made me a heart disease sufferer for life. Then there was remission and then a relapse, and then the long path to recovery began, which took as much energy as the disease itself," she says.

Many girls around the world share experiences similar to Varvara's. The teenage years are "a particularly risky time for eating disorder development in girls," says Christine Peat, a professor of psychiatry and the director of the National Center of Excellence for Eating Disorders, an organization that provides education and awareness on eating disorders and their treatment. "Everything from hormonal changes to cultural and societal pressures converge around that period of time, which can increase eating disorder risk."

Varvara is on a path of recovery, bolstered by her family's love and support. "Of course, the Snake periodically visits me, but we have built a solid defense, where everyone [in my family has] laid a brick," she writes. "That is why, looking in the mirror now, I cannot say that I like everything (it never will be so, because this infection is for life), but I love myself, and you will never kill anyone you love." ◊

*Translated from Russian*

*April 11*

The alarm clock went off at 5:15 a.m., interrupting my already short sleep. I got up dissatisfied as much as possible: the head was splitting because I had been reading the works of Old Russian literature all night, the body was broken, and I felt bad because lately I haven't had enough time to do everything. I went out to the balcony, smoked my first cigarette of the day, and cheered up. This morning everything went wrong: I almost broke a hair curler, there were traffic jams (as if in Moscow, I swear), and my stomach rumbled all day, since I did not have time to eat. I saw Chris's depressed face (table partner in school, friend) and realized that I was not the only one in such a mood :) .

Then there was a lecture on sociology, where V.V. again assured us that the world was mired in unbelief and vices, and the only salvation of mankind was in appeal to the Creator. And at the proseminar I didn't nearly fall off my chair when I heard the phrase "the main goal of a woman is to sell herself more expensive . . ." And these are thoughts of a man respected not only in close scientific circles of Saransk, but also abroad! I wanted to argue, but I changed my mind: last time I tried desperately to convince him and failed. Chris and I didn't go to the pool today which was my fault—the headache didn't go away.

When I came home, I simply fell on the bed, having slept for three hours, no less. I got up, hugged Max (damn, he came home from work, but I didn't even notice: I was so deeply immersed in the kingdom of Morpheus), asked how he was doing, made a strong coffee and went again into battle. Closer to the night I became calmer, my thoughts a little ordered. Before going to bed, I went out on the balcony and I caught an incredible thrill from the smell of spring. I remembered that my sister was arriving soon; it warmed my soul. I lay down around two o'clock in the morning, and I finally fell asleep without even thinking about what a clumsy and lazy person I was.

✳ ✳ ✳

*April 12*

A-A-A-A! Again this stupid alarm clock woke me up at 4 a.m. Surprisingly, I stood up cheerful and loving the whole world.

Today promises to be good: there will be classes with my favorite teachers (I am going to spend almost the whole day studying literature), the sun shines bright, and my beloved sister will arrive in the evening. I had a class in Old Russian literature, and incidentally, as always, it went perfectly well! The teacher is an amazing woman who will charge even the last whiner with a positive outlook, and will also enrich us with knowledge, sing, and dance right during the class! Incidentally, I promised to write an article for her before the end of the semester . . . Hmm, apparently, the writing of the work is postponed for the summer months. I feel terribly bad! I will go to her, talk on this subject, but first I will turn in the texts. Then there was a sweetheart teacher, she teaches us ancient literature. I loved to look for allusions to myths in works. And finally, my beloved S.P., who teaches, perhaps, my favorite subject—literary criticism. I, enchanted, sit at her lectures, listening to her singing voice telling us about the literary process and what great people were writers!

We didn't get to the pool again . . . This time, Kristina's head ached so much that even she, having not skipped a single time (!!!) for a whole year, asked to go home. Max took me from the university and we went home. On the way home we jumped into the store to buy groceries for a week. How I love to wander through the grocery department of the supermarket! I need everything: cinnamon in coffee, and some kind of seaweed, and some kind of green-yellow-red fruit, and pasta of all varieties (I have some kind of mania, which is expressed in the fact that I need pasta of all forms and sizes; I especially love "bows" and "cars"). Thank God, there is Max, who every time saves our budget from the next "bows" and seaweed :) . Then I had to go to the airport.

My mood abruptly changed from excellent to terrible. I felt some kind of weakness. I went to the balcony and just burst into tears. Hateful thoughts "woke up" again. Again I could not get past the mirror without seeing a fat cow. The anxiety began to grow and I, knowing that things would only get worse, went to bed. I did not meet my sister, saying that we will see each other tomorrow. I did not want to spoil either her or Mother's mood.

I do not know exactly, but, in my opinion, it was 8 p.m., no later. Even without wishing Max a good sleep, I simply fell down on the sofa, covered myself with the blanket, and fell asleep.

# Viona

## 15
### years old

Kieni, Kenya

**What are your favorite subjects?**
English, chemistry, and history

**What do you like to do outside of school?**
When I am not at school I really
like spending time reading novels.

**Tell us about your friends.**
I have many friends; my friends are endless. [Some of]
my friends' names are Everchristine, Dorecen, Mercy, and
Lindah. I really like spending time with them in school and
outside school. I have known my friends since I was young.

## "When I grow up I would like to be a news anchor and also a fashion designer."

**VIONA HAS BIG DREAMS.**

"When I grow up I would like to be a news anchor and also a fashion designer," she says. She's a girl scout and a voracious reader, and she spends a lot of her time outside school reading novels.

Viona lives with her mother, her sister, and her grandmother. Her mother is single parent who works long days as a tailor to support her small family. Her mother also, like many other people in their village, does a little farming. She has a small piece of land that she plants with beans and maize (corn).

"She is a hardworking woman. She was hustling each and every day, and sometimes I could not even see her in the morning," says Viona.

During primary school, Viona lived at home in her village of Kieni, but now, she goes to high school in a nearby town and lives in a dormitory when school is in session.

Viona shared diary entries from when she was back home during a break and writes about spending time with friends, going to church, and reading books. ◊

**IN A FEW** of her diary entries, safety concerns loom in the background—Viona writes about being thankful to reach home before dark and about walking a friend home. When I asked her about this, she listed all the dangers she encounters on the road after dark: people who might attack girls, thieves and robbers, and also hyenas that might target humans. All of this means she tries to get home quickly, and before dark, whenever possible.

There is a universality to this type of fear: on country roads and city streets across the world, women and girls fear the walk home, and the possibility of danger they could encounter in the dark. In 2011, a study conducted across 143 countries found that only 62 percent of women said they felt safe walking in their communities at night. This number dropped to 54 percent in sub-Saharan Africa.[113] This fear is only heightened by how widespread gender-based violence is in Kenya. Gender-based violence includes violence or abuse based on someone's gender identity, existing gender norms, or gender-based unequal power relationships. It can include physical violence, sexual abuse, or emotional or psychological

Kieni,
Kenya

violence or abuse. In Kenya, 47 percent of women have reported experiencing physical or sexual violence, according to the 2014 Kenya Demographic and Household Survey.[114]

This is why girls like Viona run home before darkness falls. ◊

233

*April 19, 2019*

Today is Friday, I spent my day cleaning the house and the compound. My day was quite good and enjoyable. I liked everything I did.

Today I met one of my friends by the name Everchristine who studies at Kiene high school. I had really missed her; that's why I tried my best to meet her. I was looking forward to finishing reading my novel today which [I have] been reading for the last two weeks titled *The Pearl*. I was most worried today that my mother would come from job late at night because it is a market day so I peeled some bananas for supper in case my mum would come late. I had woke up at 4:00 a.m. for my personal studies and I will go to bed at 10:00 p.m. I spent my day with my friends; I could not manage to spend my day with my family because they were all busy. I really loved my day.

✳ ✳ ✳

*April 21, 2019*

Today is a Sunday. I spent my day in church. I woke very early in the morning and washed the utensils that we had used for supper and went in the bathroom and took a warm shower. I dressed for church and left.

I left the church at one o'clock. I wanted to go to town but when I reached home, my mother told me to wash for her clothes before I leave. I did it quickly and left; on my way I met my friend and walked with her.

I did not spend my time a lot in town because I wanted to go home early to prepare supper.

On my way back home, I saw an accident and assisted the victims and because of this I was late but from there I went running and managed to be at home before darkness fell. I prepared supper and ate with my family happily. I really loved the day.

※ ※ ※

*April 22, 2019*

Today is a Monday. I spent my day cleaning the house and our compound.

Today I visited my friend who is admitted in the hospital by the name Limiar. She is Nigerian. We met each other in my former school. I took her soup and a meal for which she was very happy.

Then I went back home; on my way I met my friends whom I had not seen for long and I spent my time to talk to them. One of my friends decided to come to our home with me; when we reached home my mother asked me to prepare lunch. My friend assisted and I was very happy for that.

In the evening, my neighbour's girl came at our home asking me to plait her hair but I told her that it is very late. We escorted my friend with her, we went talking stories, cracking jokes and laughing heartily. I really loved the day.

*Thank you to WAAW Foundation and their fellows for connecting me with Viona.*

# Afterword

AS I PUT TOGETHER THIS BOOK, I thought often about how rarely we get to see the world through girls' eyes. And of how familiar it all looked, even when featuring places I had never visited, cultures that were foreign to me, or circumstances I had never lived through.

There were a few different themes that kept coming up, that perhaps many of our teenage years are defined by: the tug of curiosity and adventure and the big bad world out there, just waiting to be explored; the excitement and loneliness of moving to new places; the dread of endless days that all look the same; the struggle to feel like you fit in and are seen; the world telling you that you aren't enough or right or good, that you should take up less space; that feeling of being at the cusp of something big as you plot dreams late into the night.

And at twenty-nine, far from my own teenage girlhood, I found myself turning to these diary entries for comfort and reassurance.

These are the things that I wish I had read about when I was growing up and that I wish we talked about more in our cultures. About what life looks like for us and for everyone else.

So wherever you are, whatever your life looks like: I hope you have enjoyed seeing the world through girls' eyes and that you recognized pieces of yourself in this book, too. ◊

# Acknowledgments

**THANK YOU TO ALL THE GIRLS** who so generously shared their stories with me.

Thank you to Elise Howard, who saw a book in my series, and was the best advocate and editor for this book I could have asked for.

To my agents, Sonali Chanchani and Claudia Cross, for always championing me and my ideas, and for making sure I never felt alone in this process.

To Amy King and Neema Roshania Patel, my editors at *The Lily*, for believing in this series and giving it a platform.

Thank you to Krestyna Lypen and the entire team at Algonquin for making this book what it is.

There are so many more people than I can list who helped me along the way and helped make this book real. But here are a few:

So many people—near strangers and old friends—connected me with friends and organizations and girls they knew around the world. This book couldn't have happened without you. Thank you to Karin Joseph, Meghana Nallajerla, Helen Liu, Esha Chatterjee, Jacarand Joshi, Renu Brij, Rachel Schallom, Shanika Perera, Sabina Carlson, Edoardo Borgomeo, Josie Messa, Julia Carpenter, Cristina Osorio, Sharonya Vadakattu, Amruta Byatnal, Kari Cobham, and Kristina Budelis.

To the friends who have been sounding boards, cheerleaders, and endless sources of support—the people I text from the other side of the world and whose couches I know I can always crash on: Sally Dickinson, Emily Chow, Elite Truong, Dhiya Kuriakose-Gerber, Katie Park, Lucy Arora, Vindhya Buthpitiya, Kassy Cho, Aditi Bhandari, Denise Lu, Kate Parkinson-Morgan, Sam Schlinkert, Ruwangi Amarasinghe, Sanora Rodrigo, Ram Joshi, and Matt Rattley.

The friends who are creative accountability partners and trusted sounding boards: Kat Chow, Alex Laughlin, John Sutter, Phoebe Connelly, Katie Hawkins-Gaar, and Jen Mizgata.

Thank you to the editors who believed in me before I did, who taught me how to be a journalist and have always rooted for me: Mary Jordan, Steven Ginsberg, and Cory Haik.

To the editors who said yes to my weird ideas and gave me space to find my voice: Sam Barry, Ashley Codianni, and Caroline Paterson.

This book was written in motion, across countries and continents, on friends' couches and in spare rooms. Thank you to everyone who opened their doors to me, particularly Purvi and Gaurang and Venkatesh Uncle, Saras Aunty, Nalini, and Saumya.

And to my brother Uthsav and my parents. Thank you for everything. None of this could be real without you. ◊

# Notes

**INTRODUCTION**

1 "Child Marriage," United Nations Population Fund, 2018, https://www.unfpa.org/child-marriage.

2 Jones, Coby. "Every Day 41,000 Girls Are Married Under the Age of 18. A New World Bank Report Shows the Economic Impact of This Problem," *UN Dispatch*, July 12, 2017, https://www.undispatch.com/every-day-41000-girls-married-age-18-new-world-bank-report-shows-economic-impact-problem/.

3 *Girlhood, Not Motherhood: Preventing Adolescent Pregnancy*, United Nations Population Fund, New York, 2015, https://www.unfpa.org/sites/default/files/pub-pdf/Girlhood_not_motherhood_final_web.pdf.

4 "Girls' Education," The World Bank, September 25, 2017, https://www.worldbank.org/en/topic/girlseducation.

5 McCoy, Terrence. "Child Marriage in the U.S. Is Surprisingly Prevalent. Now States Are Passing Laws to Make It Harder," *Washington Post*, October 10, 2018, https://www.washingtonpost.com/news/national/wp/2018/10/05/feature/child-marriage-in-the-u-s-is-surprisingly-prevalent-now-states-are-passing-laws-to-make-it-harder/.

**ALEJANDRA**

6 "Argentines Protest Violence Against Women in Large Marches,"*AP News*, June 3, 2019, https://apnews.com/15bb663b4c034af8827e421ac450c504.

7 "Femicide Is Everybody's Issue—Argentina, EU and UN Team Up to End Violence Against Women and Girls," International Cooperation and Development, May 22, 2019, https://ec.europa.eu/europeaid/news-and-events/femicide-everybodys-issue-argentina-eu-and-un-team-end-violence-against-women-and_en.

8 Soto, Isabella. "INDEC: Complaints of Gender-Based Violence Quadrupled in Just Five Years," *Buenos Aires Times*, August 3, 2018, https://www.batimes.com.ar/news/argentina/complaints-of-gender-based-violence-quadrupled-in-argentina-indec.phtml.

**AMIYA**

9 "What Does the 2011 Census Tell Us About Inter-Ethnic Relationships?" [United Kingdom] Office for National Statistics, July 3, 2014, https://webarchive.nationalarchives.gov.uk/20160107132103/http://www.ons.gov.uk/ons/dcp171776_369571.pdf

10 " 'We've Always Had a Seat at the Table': Solange on Conversations That Heal," NPR, November 11, 2016, https://www.npr.org/2016/11/11/501165834/weve-always-had-a-seat-at-the-table-solange-on-conversations-that-heal.

**ANNA**

11 Woodgate, Thomas. "15 Best Sydney Beaches," *CNN*, 2018, https://edition.cnn.com/travel/article/sydney-best-beaches/index html.

12 "Greater Sydney—City of Sydney," City of Sydney, April 26, 2018, https://www.cityofsydney.nsw.gov.au/learn/research-and-statistics/the-city-at-a-glance/greater-sydney.

[13] "Sydney Languages," *Sydney Morning Herald*, July 12, 2014, https://www.smh.com.au/interactive/2014/sydney-languages/.

## AYAULYM

[14] "18 Thousand Foreign Students Study at Kazakhstan's Universities in 2018," *Qazaq Times*, October 17, 2018, https://qazaqtimes.com/en/article/49355.

[15] Shayakhmetova, Zhanna. "International Students Say They Appreciate Studies, Life in Kazakhstan," *Edge: Kazakhstan*, 2019, https://www.edgekz.com/international-students-say-appreciate-studies-life-kazakhstan/.

[16] "Kazakhstan Country Profile," *BBC News*, August 9, 2019, https://www.bbc.co.uk/news/world-asia-pacific-15263826.

[17] The World Economic Forum, *Global Gender Gap Report*, 2017, http://www3.weforum.org/docs/WEF_GGGR_2017.pdf.

## CHANLEAKNA

[18] *General Population Census of the Kingdom of Cambodia*, National Institute of Statistics, Ministry of Planning, June 2019, https://www.nis.gov.kh/nis/Census2019/Provisional%20Population%20Census%202019_English_FINAL.pdf

[19] "Cambodia Youth Data Sheet 2015," United Nations Population Fund, February 25, 2016, https://cambodia.unfpa.org/sites/default/files/pub-pdf/Flyer_Cambodia_Youth_Factsheet_final_draft_%28approved%29.pdf.

[20] Ibid.

[21] "The State of International Student Mobility in 2015," *ICEF Monitor*, November 5, 2015, https://monitor.icef.com/2015/11/the-state-of-international-student-mobility-in-2015/.

[22] "International Student Data: Monthly Summary," Australian Government Department of Education, July 2019, https://internationaleducation.gov.au/research/International-Student-Data/Documents/MONTHLY%20SUMMARIES/2019/Jul%202019%20MonthlyInfographic.pdf

[23] Ibid.

## CHEN XI

[24] Population Singapore: "Demographics," 2018, https://www.population.sg/articles/population-in-brief-2019-what-do-you-need-to-know.

[25] Coughlan, Sean. "Singapore First Place in School Rankings," BBC News, December 6, 2016, https://www.bbc.co.uk/news/education-38212070.

[26] Davie, Sandra. "Singapore Students Suffer From High Levels of Anxiety: Study," *Straits Times*, August 20, 2017, https://www.straitstimes.com/singapore/education/spore-students-suffer-from-high-levels-of-anxiety-study.

## CLAUDIE

[27] Winterman, Denise. "What's So Great About Living in Vanuatu?" BBC, July 13, 2006, http://news.bbc.co.uk/1/hi/magazine/5172254.stm.

[28] Cullwick, Jonas. "Enact 50% Quota For Women in Parliament," *Vanuatu Daily Post*, May 16, 2018, http://dailypost.vu/news/enact-quota-for-women-in-parliament/article_ff89b1e1-a675-57ec-b791-3f950eeee19d.html.

[29] "New Pacific Partnership Addresses Gender Equality and Violence Against Women," European External Action Service, November 26, 2018, https://eeas.europa.eu/sites/eeas/files/download_evawg_pacp_launch_media_release.pdf.

## DESIREÉ

[30] "Number of Population Estimated by Nationality—Emirate of Dubai," Dubai Statistics Center, 2015–2017, https://www.dsc.gov.ae/Report/DSC_SYB_2017_01%20_%2003.pdf.

[31] Youha, Ali Al, and Froilan T. Malit. "Labor Migration in the United Arab Emirates: Challenges and Responses," Migration Policy Institute, September 18, 2013, https://www.migrationpolicy.org/article/labor-migration-united-arab-emirates-challenges-and-responses.

[32] "World Report 2019: Rights Trends in United Arab Emirates," *Human Rights Watch*, 2019, https://www.hrw.org/world-report/2019/country-chapters/united-arab-emirates.

## DIZA

[33] Chakravarty, Manas. "Richest 10% of Indians Own Over 3/4th of Wealth in India," *Live Mint*, October 23, 2018, https://www.livemint.com/Money/iH2aBEUDpG06hM78diSSEJ/Richest-10-of-Indians-own-over-34th-of-wealth-in-India.html.

[34] Bhattacharya, Ananya. "India Will Have Nearly a Million Millionaires by 2027," *Quartz India*, June 28, 2018, https://qz.com/india/1316124/india-will-have-nearly-a-million-millionaires-by-2027/.

[35] Bhattacharya, Ananya. "Mapped: In India's Wealthiest City, the Ultra-Rich and Slum Dwellers Share Neighbourhoods," *Quartz India*, October 28, 2019, https://qz.com/india/1729770/in-mumbai-the-ultra-rich-and-slum-dwellers-share-neighbourhoods/.

## EMILLY

[36] Barbara, Vanessa. "Brazil's Unaffordable Homes," *New York Times*, July 31, 2014, https://www.nytimes.com/2014/07/31/opinion/vanessa-barbara-brazils-unaffordable-homes.html.

[37] Ortiz, Erik. "What Is a Favela? Five Things to Know about Rio's So-Called Shantytowns," *NBC News*, August 4, 2016, https://www.nbcnews.com/storyline/2016-rio-summer-olympics/what-favela-five-things-know-about-rio-s-so-called-n622836.

[38] Barcelos, Iuri, and Natalia Viana. "Revealed: Fires in São Paulo Favelas More Likely on Higher-Value Land," *Guardian*, November 27, 2017, https://www.theguardian.com/cities/2017/nov/27/revealed-fires-sao-paulo-favelas-higher-value-land.

[39] "Brazil's Ministry of Health: One in Five Children Born to Adolescent Moms," *CGTN*, March 27, 2017, https://news.cgtn.com/news/3d41544f77497a4d/share_p.html.

[40] Moreno, Ana Carolina, and Gabriela Gonçalves. "No Brasil, 75% Das Adolescentes Que Têm Filhos Estão Fora da Escola," *Educação*, March 31, 2015, http://g1.globo.com/educacao/noticia/2015/03/no -brasil-75-das-adolescentes-que-tem-filhos-estao-fora-da-escola.html.

[41] "Adolescent Pregnancy," World Health Organization, January 31, 2020, https://www.who.int/news -room/fact-sheets/detail/adolescent-pregnancy.

## FAVOUR

[42] "'Millions of Nigerian Children' Out of School," *BBC News*, July 25, 2017, https://www.bbc.co.uk /news/world-africa-40715305.

[43] "Education | UNICEF Nigeria," Unicef.org, 2019, https://www.unicef.org/nigeria/education.

[44] "Boko Haram Fast Facts," CNN, June 9, 2019, https://edition.cnn.com/2014/06/09/world/boko -haram-fast-facts/index.html.

[45] Ibid.

[46] Sieff, Kevin. "82 Chibok Girls Freed in Nigeria after Years in Boko Haram Custody," *Washington Post*, May 6, 2017, https://www.washingtonpost.com/world/82-chibok-girls-freed-in-nigeria-after-years -in-boko-haram-custody/2017/05/06/34865c84-a398-4af9-90e5-1baafea4f23d_story.html

[47] UNICEF. "More than 1,000 Children in Northeastern Nigeria Abducted by Boko Haram since 2013," April 13, 2018, https://www.unicef.org/wca/press-releases/more-1000-children-northeastern -nigeria-abducted-boko-haram-2013.

[48] Maclean, Ruth, and Isaac Abrak. "Boko Haram Returns More than 100 Schoolgirls Kidnapped Last Month," *Guardian*, March 21, 2018, https://www.theguardian.com/world/2018/mar/21/boko -haram-returns-some-of-the-girls-it-kidnapped-last-month.

## HALIMA

[49] Mellen, Ruby. "Afghanistan Ranks among the Worst Places for Girls to Get an Education," October 17, 2017, https://foreignpolicy.com/2017/10/17/afghanistan-ranks-worst-places-girls-to-get-an -education-africa/.

[50] "Women in Afghanistan: The Back Story," Amnesty International, UK, November 25, 2014, https:// www.amnesty.org.uk/womens-rights-afghanistan-history.

[51] Gibbons-Neff, Thomas. "Attacks by Extremists on Afghan Schools Triple, Report Says," *New York Times*, May 27, 2019, https://www.nytimes.com/2019/05/27/world/asia/afghanistan-attacks-schools -unicef.html.

[52] Human Rights Watch. "'I Won't Be a Doctor, and One Day You'll Be Sick': Girls' Access to Education in Afghanistan," Human Rights Watch, October 17, 2017, https://www.hrw.org/report /2017/10/17/i-wont-be-doctor-and-one-day-youll-be-sick/girls-access-education-afghanistan.

[53] "Afghanistan: Girls Struggle for an Education," Human Rights Watch, October 17, 2017, https:// www.hrw.org/news/2017/10/17/afghanistan-girls-struggle-education.

[54] Human Rights Watch.

## JOCELYNE

[55] "Overview: Democratic Republic of Congo," World Bank, 2019, https://www.worldbank.org/en /country/drc/overview.

[56] Bearak, Max. "Caught in Congo's Tides of War," *Washington Post*, April 6, 2018, https://www .washingtonpost.com/graphics/2018/world/dr-congo-conflict-uganda-refugee-crisis/.

[57] Burke, Jason. " 'The Wars Will Never Stop'—Millions Flee Bloodshed as Congo Falls Apart," *Guardian*, April 3, 2018, https://www.theguardian.com/world/2018/apr/03/millions-flee-bloodshed-as -congos-army-steps-up-fight-with-rebels-in-east.

[58] Knapp Sawyer, Kem, and Sawyer, Jon. "Congo's Children," *Atavist*, 2014, https://pulitzercenter .atavist.com/webcongoschildren.

[59] Oritz, Fabiola. " 'They Told Me I Would Be a Soldier': The DRC Conflict's Forgotten Girls," *News Deeply*, January 8, 2018, https://www.newsdeeply.com/womenandgirls/articles/2018/01/08/they-told -me-i-would-be-a-soldier-the-drc-conflicts-forgotten-girls.

[60] Bearak, Max. "Caught in Congo's Tides of War."

[61] Burke, Jason. "'The Wars Will Never Stop'—Millions Flee Bloodshed as Congo Falls Apart."

[62] "Q&A: DR Congo Conflict," *BBC News*, November 20, 2012, https://www.bbc.co.uk/news/world -africa-11108589.

## LUCIANA

[63] Destination Imagination: "Our Statistics," 2020, https://www.destinationimagination.org/our-stats/.

[64] Jordan, Miriam. "More Migrants Are Crossing the Border This Year. What's Changed?" *New York Times*, March 5, 2019, https://www.nytimes.com/2019/03/05/us/crossing-the-border-statistics.html.

[65] Guinan, Julie. "Nearly 20 Years after Peace Pact, Guatemala's Women Relive Violence," CNN, April 8, 2015, https://edition.cnn.com/2015/04/02/world/iyw-guatemala-gender-violence/index.html.

[66] World Bank: "Poverty and Equity Brief: Guatemala," 2019, http://povertydata.worldbank.org /poverty/country/GTM

[67] Leutert, Stephanie. "Why Are So Many Migrants Leaving Guatemala? A Crisis in the Coffee Industry Is One Reason," *Time*, July 27, 2018, https://time.com/5346110/guatemala-coffee-escape-migration/.

[68] Blitzer, Jonathan. "How Climate Change Is Fuelling the U.S. Border Crisis," *New Yorker*, April 3, 2019, https://www.newyorker.com/news/dispatch/how-climate-change-is-fuelling-the-us-border-crisis.

[69] "The World Bank in Guatemala." October 10, 2019, https://www.worldbank.org/en/country /guatemala/overview.

## MANDISA

[70] "Adolescent Pregnancy," United Nations Population Fund, 2019, https://www.unfpa.org /adolescent-pregnancy.

[71] *Leave No Girl Behind in Africa: Discrimination in Education Against Pregnant Girls and Adolescent Mothers.* Human Rights Watch, June 2018, https://www.hrw.org/sites/default/files/report _pdf/au0618_insert_webspreads.pdf

[72] Ibid.

## MARTA

[73] "Milan," World Cities Culture Forum, 2020, http://www.worldcitiescultureforum.com/cities/milan/.

[74] Coman, Julian. "How the Megacities of Europe Stole a Continent's Wealth," *Guardian*, November 10, 2019, https://www.theguardian.com/cities/2019/nov/10/how-europes-cities-stole-continents-wealth.

## MARISENA

[75] *The World Factbook*, "Haiti," Central Intelligence Agency, 2019, https://www.cia.gov/library/publications/the-world-factbook/geos/ha.html.

[76] Ibid.

[77] "Haiti Earthquake Fast Facts," *CNN*, December 12, 2018, https://www.cnn.com/2013/12/12/world/haiti-earthquake-fast-facts/index.html.

[78] "UN Admits Role in Haiti Cholera Outbreak," *BBC News*, August 19, 2016, https://www.bbc.co.uk/news/world-latin-america-37126747.

[79] Thomassaint Joseph, Ralph. "Without Venezuela's Oil, Haiti Struggles to Keep Lights On," AP News, May 17, 2019, https://apnews com/1f261ed6fc964244af509cf09ed0a863.

## MIRIAM

[80] United Nations Development Programme, "Gender Inequality Index," *Human Development Reports*, 2017, http://hdr.undp.org/en/composite/GII.

[81] "Country Ranking," *Rainbow Europe*, 2019, https://rainbow-europe.org/country-ranking.

[82] Bränström, Richard. *The Health and Situation of Young LGBTQ People in Sweden—What Do We Know and Where Is More Research Needed?* Forte: Swedish Research Council for Health, Working Life, and Welfare, 2019, https://forte.se/en/publication/health-situation-young-lgbtq-people-sweden-know-research-needed/.

[83] "Out Online: The Experiences of Lesbian, Gay, Bisexual and Transgender Youth," GLSEN, July 10, 2013, https://www.glsen.org/news/out-online-experiences-lgbt-youth-internet

## NAYA

[84] "Figures at a Glance: Statistical Yearbooks," UN Refugee Agency, 2019, https://www.unhcr.org/uk/figures-at-a-glance.html.

[85] "Child Displacement," UNICEF Data, December 2018, https://data.unicef.org/topic/child-migration-and-displacement/migration/.

## RAKSA

[86] "WFP Cambodia Country Brief," World Food Programme, June 2019, https://docs.wfp.org/api/documents/WFP-0000106853/download/?_ga=2.165748030.1677689029.1564432037-1244524808.1563636734.

[87] Ibid.

[88] "The World Bank in Cambodia," World Bank, 2019. https://www.worldbank.org/en/country/cambodia/overview.

## RUKSAR

[89] Saldanha, Alison. "India's Richest Young Women Fear Public Transport Most; Poorest Fear Cinema Halls," *IndiaSpend*, July 2, 2018, https://www.indiaspend.com/indias-richest-young-women-fear-public-transport-most-poorest-fear-cinema-halls-52916/.

[90] Doshi, Vidhi. " 'What Is Rape, Mom?': A Small Town in India Grapples with How to Protect Children," *Washington Post*, July 23, 2018, https://www.washingtonpost.com/world/asia_pacific/what-is-rape-mom-a-small-town-in-india-grapples-with-how-to-protect-children/2018/07/23/e01b5000-4e1c-11e8-85c1-9326c4511033_story.html.

[91] Kundu, Tadit, and Pramit Bhattacharya. "99% Cases of Sexual Assaults Go Unreported, Govt Data Shows," *Live Mint*, April 24, 2018, https://www.livemint.com/PoliticsAV3sIK0EBAGZozALMX8THK/99-cases-of-sexual-assaults-go-unreported-govt-data-shows.html.

[92] Gowen, Annie. "India Has 63 Million 'Missing' Women and 21 Million Unwanted Girls, Government Says," *Washington Post*, April 24, 2018, https://www.washingtonpost.com/news/worldviews/wp/2018/01/29/india-has-63-million-missing-women-and-21-million-unwanted-girls-government-says/.

[93] Ibid.

## RUOXIAO

[94] Fifield, Anna. "Beijing's One-Child Policy Is Gone. But Many Chinese Are Still Reluctant to Have More," *Washington Post*, May 2, 2019, https://www.washingtonpost.com/world/asia_pacific/beijings-one-child-policy-is-gone-but-many-chinese-are-still-reluctant-to-have-more/2019/05/02/c722e568-604f-11e9-bf24-db4b9fb62aa2_story.html.

[95] Denyer, Simon, and Annie Gowen. "Too Many Men," *Washington Post*, April 18, 2018, https://www.washingtonpost.com/graphics/2018/world/too-many-men/.

[96] Zraick, Karen. "China Will Feel One-Child Policy's Effects for Decades, Experts Say," *New York Times*, October 30, 2015, https://www.nytimes.com/2015/10/31/world/asia/china-will-feel-one-child-policys-effects-for-decades-experts-say.html.

[97] Denyer, Simon, and Annie Gowen. "Too Many Men."

## RUQAYA

[98] "Guide: What's Happening in Iraq?" *BBC Newsround*. November 29, 2016, https://www.bbc.co.uk/newsround/27868389.

[99] "Iraq—Child Marriage Around the World," *Girls Not Brides*, 2019, https://www.girlsnotbrides.org/child-marriage/iraq/.

## SATTIGUL

[100] Trankmann, Beate. "Nomads No More," United Nations Development Programme, September 25, 2018, https://www.undp.org/content/undp/en/home/blog/2018/Nomads-no-more.html.

[101] Kingsley, Patrick. "Nomads No More: Why Mongolian Herders Are Moving to the City," *Guardian*, January 5, 2017, https://www.theguardian.com/world/2017/jan/05/mongolian-herders-moving-to-city-climate-change.

[102] Trankmann, Beate. "Nomads No More."

## SHANAI

[103] Roberts, Sam. "The Lost Languages, Found in New York," *New York Times*, April 29, 2010, https://www.nytimes.com/2010/04/29/nyregion/29lost.html.

[104] "100 Women: How Hollywood Fails Women on Screen," *BBC News*, March 2, 2018, https://www.bbc.co.uk/news/world-43197774.

## SOFIA

[105] "Panama," Panama Wildlife Conservation, 2019, https://panamawildlife.org/about-panama/.

[106] Wearden, Graeme. "More Plastic than Fish in the Sea by 2050, Says Ellen MacArthur," *Guardian*, January 19, 2016, https://www.theguardian.com/business/2016/jan/19/more-plastic-than-fish-in-the-sea-by-2050-warns-ellen-macarthur.

[107] "Adapting to Climate Change through Integrated Water Management in Panama," Adaptation Fund, 2019, https://www.adaptation-fund.org/project/adapting-climate-change-integrated-water-management-panama/.

[108] *Climate Change in Central America: Potential Impacts and Public Policy Options*, United Nations, 2018. https://repositorio.cepal.org/bitstream/handle/11362/39150/7/S1800827_en.pdf.

## SOPHIE

[109] Horowitz, Juliana Menasce. "Most U.S. Teens See Anxiety, Depression as Major Problems," Pew Research Center: *Social & Demographic Trends*, February 20, 2019, https://www.pewsocialtrends.org/2019/02/20/most-u-s-teens-see-anxiety-and-depression-as-a-major-problem-among-their-peers/.

[110] Snow, Kate, and Cynthia McFadden. "Generation at Risk: America's Youngest Facing Mental Health Crisis," *NBC News*, December 10, 2017, https://www.nbcnews.com/health/kids-health/generation-risk-america-s-youngest-facing-mental-health-crisis-n827836.

[111] Cha, Ariana Eungjung. "More than a Third of Teenage Girls Experience Depression, New Study Says," *Washington Post*, May 31, 2017, https://www.washingtonpost.com/news/to-your-health/wp/2017/05/31/more-than-a-third-of-teenage-girls-experience-depression-new-study-says/.

[112] Horowitz, Juliana Menasce. "Most U.S. Teens See Anxiety, Depression as Major Problems."

## VIONA

[113] Crabtree, Steve, and Faith Nsubuga. "Women Feel Less Safe than Men in Many Developed Countries," *Gallup*, July 26, 2012, https://news.gallup.com/poll/155402/women-feel-less-safe-men-developed-countries.aspx.

[114] Otewa, Faith. "Looking at Gender Based Violence in Kenya," The Center for Global Reproductive Health at Duke, January 18, 2019, http://dukecenterforglobalreproductivehealth.org/2019/01/18/looking-at-gender-based-violence-in-kenya/.

Kassy Cho

**MASUMA AHUJA** is a journalist who calls three countries home and reports on people, power, and politics around the world. Her work focuses primarily on women's and girls' lives. She was previously a producer at CNN and national digital editor at the *Washington Post*. She uses words, photos, and emerging media to report and tell stories. Her projects have ranged from long-form stories to sending disposable cameras to women in more than a dozen countries to document their days to crowdsourcing voice mails from Americans about the impact of the 2016 election on their lives. She was part of a team that won the Pulitzer Prize in 2014.